# Endorsements

As a former public education leader, principal, and educator—and now the founder of a school—I can say with conviction that Dr. Ivy Bonk's work is essential for the future of education. Her framework is not simply an academic exercise; it is a blueprint for transformation that we must urgently embrace if we want to see lasting success in the lives of our students.

Dr. Bonk has masterfully integrated rigorous research with a profound understanding of the spiritual and emotional dimensions of learning, bridging a gap that is too often ignored in our systems. Her ability to connect education with the wholeness of the individual is both refreshing and necessary. *Education's Reset and A Society's Healing* is not only a book—it is a movement, and I am honored to be partnering with Dr. Bonk to mobilize this work in schools.

Every educator, policymaker, and leader invested in the next generation should read this book and take its message to heart.

*Dr. Darius Williams*
*Reformation Academy*

At the core of Dr. Bonk's work is a deep commitment to unlocking the potential within every student—a mission that resonates strongly with my own. I have witnessed, time and again across diverse settings and cultures, how children previously labeled or constrained by diagnoses can become suddenly and profoundly "unlocked" when met by an educator or provider who holds space with both compassion and high expectations. Dr. Bonk's vision in *Education's Reset and a Society's Healing* is both timely and inspiring, and I am genuinely excited about its implications for the future of children›s growth and learning.

*Dr. Kevin Spencer*
*Hocus Focus*

As a co-laborer in education with Dr. Bonk, I admire and appreciate her ability to integrate solutions across all the parts as an effort to reduce mass fragmentation on scale. As a seasoned administrator who has successfully experienced implementation of many of the strategies shared herein, I can attest to their effectiveness. When schools begin to focus on helping students understand and regulate their brains, and in response educators, students, and parents understand its connection to undesired behaviors, we will address many of the challenges we are facing in education.

*Dr. Dinorah Bores*
*School Administrator, Texas*

As a fellow social innovator and designer of an educational ecosystem (1 Million Teachers) established to bring equity-based learning to educators of Sub Saharan Africa and the children it serves, Dr. Bonk's audacious goal of remediating an entire long-established system back to equitable foundations is to be commended. Her ability and gifting to see various and diverse scenarios through the lens of trauma with the added ability to design a customized solution is one that 1 Million Teachers has benefitted from and one that we fully support.

*Hakeem Subair, Co-Founder*
*1 Million Teachers*

As a leader in Zambia, charged with serving and addressing the many needs of its young people, we are excited about adapting and integrating the foundational strategies of trauma resilience found in this writing into our systems and projects countering the effects of what we all know as a global mental health crisis.

*Permanent Secretary Fumba Chama*
*Government of Zambia, Ministry of Youth, Sports and Arts*

Equity for all students and a desire that the trauma-informed education and support provided at Generation One lead to the betterment of children's lives and the lives of their families has been at the core of our mission. The idea that other schools would adopt this social pedagogy, as outlined by Dr. Bonk, allowing us the assurance that we are sending our students to other learning environments with the same heart and intent is an overwhelming and welcoming thought.

*Mike Malkemes, Founder*
*Generation One*

As those who have long journeyed on a path, pioneering solutions to challenges that others may not fully embrace, understand, or even be aware exists, we are excited about the possibilities and alignments of sharing integration and processing solutions with those who choose to engage in education's reset and accept the charge presented by Dr. Bonk.

*Bonnie and Jamie Brandes*
*Quantum Reflex Integration*

As someone advocating for restorative justice within the criminal justice system, it is promising to know that there are those like Dr. Bonk who understand the systemic roots and can offer solutions by which we can ALL move forward.

*Dr. Taryn VanderPyl, Criminal Justice Sciences Division,*
*Western Oregon University*
*Co-Founder, Transformative Justice Community*

I spent a career in juvenile justice where I had a front row seat to the effects of a failed education system on our young people. The funnel created by the errant diagnosis and misunderstandings of those coming from historically marginalized communities filled my every day. I watched the emotional and psychological weight of wrong messaging lived out in the physical outcomes of these young people knowing in my heart they were capable of and made for so much more. The inequity this creates demands our full attention. *Education's Reset and a Society's Healing* is a recommended read for anyone charged with the honor of nurturing and caring for our children and students.

*Sedrick Wilson, Retired*
*Alabama Administrative Office of Courts*

# EDUCATION'S RESET AND A SOCIETY'S HEALING

GO UPSTREAM. REESTABLISH FOUNDATIONS. HEAL A NATION.

ARCHITECT OF THE UNIVERSAL EQUITY PEDAGOGY

**DR. IVY BONK**

Every Child Whole Press
ISBN: 978-0-9882404-3-8

# ACKNOWLEDGEMENT

I thank God for the journey, for the gift box of brokenness that when healed reveals precious jewels, mosaics, and steppingstones. The kind of jewels, mosaics, and steppingstones that repair breaches and rebuild streets.

# DEDICATION

To Harper Lynn and Makenna Reese, may it never be that someone's observation of what they perceive to be your limited capacity, ever keep you from what God has deemed your true abilities.

# CONTENTS

# PREFACE

When we can acknowledge and recognize how injustices have been woven into structures and institutions, we can begin to clearly see and understand how humanity has arrived at its current state.

By connecting the dots provided in our country's timeline, we can begin to close the gap on an historical and generational narrative that has kept people marginalized and living well below their potential. When we innovate from within the predecessor system of education, we can interrupt the cycle of misinterpretation, misrepresentation, and misdiagnosis, and structually weaken the root of the predisposition to systems dependency and the mass causalities and lost potential found there.

**NOTE**: Examples offered in the book highlight numbers and realities specific to African-American populations. However, this does not in any way minimize similar or related events directed at other "people groups", but rather the information that is more frequently documented and shared.

If I understand your need and can meet it by bringing an answer closer to you by eliminating the need to jump through two hoops and take four extra steps, then this is what I should do. This looks like identifying possible solutions that are downstream in the system continuum, and walking them back into education—in proximity to the problem. This is called just and fair; this is called the way it should have been from the beginning; and this is called reestablishing equitable foundations in education. This is where you begin to bring order back to cataclysmic dysfunction.

We must realize that what many perceive as equity is shaped by human behavior. When individuals carry unaddressed and unresolved trauma, their responses show up as maladaptive emotions and behaviors. These maladaptive emotions and behaviors impair a person's ability to engage in equitable (others-centered) actions—making trauma not just a personal issue or challenge, but a foundational cause of inequity. It is my assertion that in order to support a reset then the reordering and reimagining is required.

To that end, the purpose of this book is fivefold and my attempt to:

1. Cut through the complex and make it simple.
2. Communicate to the reader the relationship between the micro and the macro.
3. Challenge a deficit narrative that is draining a society of much untapped potential.
4. Call processes and functions back into order.
5. Contribute a systemic solution to bring a reset to education and healing to a society.

*And yes, I do have an affinity for alliterations.*

# INTRODUCTION

**On November 6, 2024, before there was ever a signed executive order, there was a promise in a victory speech to help heal America.**

The promise of healing quickly muffled by the predictable sounds of grown men and women, commonly referred to as politicians, engaged in a *he said she said*. Each in their respective ditches or fox holes, shooting across the aisle at each other. While hungry media stood on the sidelines eager to grab a headline they could twist and use to bait you and I to trauma bond and click on through only to find ourselves fallen yet again in a ditch.

For the love of God and for the sake of our children, and in my best Bob Newhart* imitation,

## "STOP IT!"

**The Bob Newhard Show sitcom from the 70;s*

> **NOTE**: Avoidance of ditches and fox holes require the ability to lay down and step away from agendas – hidden and obvious – engaging in the present moment with active listening, compassion, and understanding directed at another person. It also requires addressing self-protective triggers manipulated when language that is not your own is used. Be cautious not to make biased accusations and prejudice declarations, rather master the art of asking questions with the intention of learning and creating context and clarity.

**America is looking for men and women that can stand in the middle of the proverbial road and not be swayed but stand, not as a matter of compromise, but as a testament and standard of truth and true equity; and nations are looking to America.**

Let us be clear, ridding ourselves of special government-funded programs – not a vote for or against – but making a point, does not rid us of the collective trauma from history. ***Oh, that it could be so simple.***

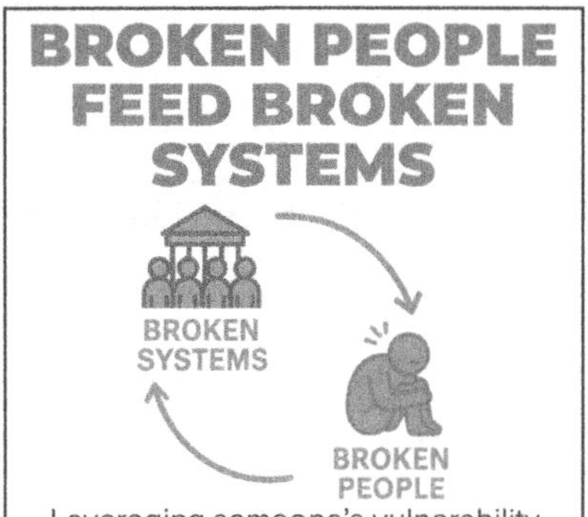

Leveraging someone's vulnerability without concern for their further detriment is bad business.

Persons overwhelmed by generations of adversity are easily manipulated by persons, programs, and systems who would like to keep them there, creating a cycle of broken systems feeding on broken people.

We must begin to understand that our response to situations and circumstances as a society is the mass result of all the fragmentation and unhealed emotions carried by the majority and accumulated over time. To be clear, majority, as in people, not a political party.

The impact of the historical and generational trauma in society has come full circle. **Our broken systems have run their course. We can't keep going the way we have been going. It is not working.** The influence of brokenness has permeated the masses and the systems in which we operate.

If we are not looking through the lens of trauma as we address the systemic challenges, then we are not looking rightly. We need well-grounded and trauma-resilient solutions that are cohesive and systemic if we are going remediate and reset, and we need them now.

We began this discussion in my first book, *Grounded Learning: Education's Recovery Plan*, which I made sure to point out was not a comprehensive map, but more of a clarion call. This book, *Education's Reset and a Society's Healing*, might be called a completed thought to the first as we are ever being informed. A completed thought, yet an abridged version of so much more. My hope is that it would be a beginning point to what lies ahead. Therefore, some of the content will be an updated refresher from the first as well as information outlined in my white paper published in 2024.

One of the repeated mentions is regarding the work of Thomas Kuhn. In his work, *The Structure for Scientific Revolutions*[1], he stated that there are two things needed to revolutionize a model: (1) Evidence that the current system isn't working anymore—but more than just "not working," it must be "not working *cataclysmically*," and (2) Availability of an alternative model.

The synergy of brokenness in people and, to use Kuhn's term, its "cataclysmic intersect" with the brokenness of our education system demands our attention. Although I don't think the "*not working cataclysmically*" part needs much discussion, *Education's Reset and a Society's* Healing speaks to an alternative. There are many models and some successful, but not at scale. They are great for those who stand to benefit, but we are not talking about another program or model only, but a systemic solution. A systemic solution that makes it possible for the different models and frameworks to thrive for the good of all. However, before we can talk about the systemic solution, we must address some of the realities that brought us to this point.

*Education's Reset and a Society's Healing* is divided into two parts. Part I addressing cause and effect; Part II, the suggestion of a counter.

---

1 Kuhn, T. S. (1962). The structure of scientific revolutions. University of Chicago Press: Chicago.

# PART I
# THE ROOT CAUSE AND ITS EFFECT

# CHAPTER ONE
# THE PROBLEM—MICRO

In this first chapter, I share my journey uncovering how deeply childhood trauma impacts learning—and how it's often misdiagnosed as a disability. I explain how trauma dysregulates the brain, causing behaviors that get misunderstood, leading to services that don't address the root issue and only deepen the cycle of failure. I introduce the **Blueprint of Trauma's Comprehensive Expression (TCE)**, showing how trauma affects the **spirit, soul, and body**, fragmenting identity and distorting our systems. This chapter is a call to action: if we want lasting educational reform, we must first focus on **healing**—both personally and collectively. Only then can we create trauma-resilient systems and unlock our full human potential.

# CHAPTER ONE
# THE PROBLEM—MICRO

It has been 17 years since I began this investigative journey. It was a spring day of 2008, and I was reviewing yet another referral for special needs testing, when I had a new thought. I happened to know the backstory of this young person whose folder I considered. He had four different sets of adults all telling him how things should be, none of which lined up with the other. My new thought? *How the hell could he not be anything but ADH/D*? *What if we were not looking at a true learning disability, but rather, we are seeing the effects of his current childhood trauma*? This new thought sent me looking for answers and two weeks later I would find myself in a doctoral program hypothesis in hand. My hypothesis? There is a direct correlation between the misdiagnosis of learning disabilities and the emotional and psychological effects of childhood trauma. The research was not available then like it is now, and I would have to create a synthesis of the research and connect my own dots. I would ask questions like; *how does trauma impact the brain? What parts of the brain does trauma impact? What are the functions needed to be successful in the classroom? What parts of the brain are connected to the functions that are needed to be successful in the classroom?* You get the idea.

Certainly, we had Dr. Bruce Perry, Dr. Gabor Mate, Dr. Bessel van der Kolk, and others but their research at the time, in my novice understanding, leaned more clinical. I was looking for solutions in education. I was looking for answers for my friend who didn't have the ability to tell me why he was having trouble paying attention and remaining focused in class. I found out that trauma alters the physical architecture of your brain impacting the very processes and supports needed to be successful in the classroom. Therefore, my dissertation would focus on five cognitive processes (integration, executive functioning, attention, memory, and language) required for learning and the impairement caused due to the emotional dysregulation from trauma.

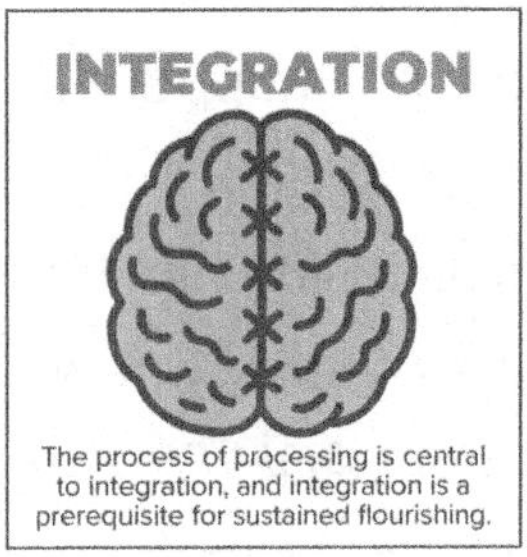

The process of processing is central to integration, and integration is a prerequisite for sustained flourishing.

To be on the top of your game, you must operate from the top of your brain.

To stay (attend) is to hold (take in and process); and to hold is to learn and heal.

The hold and recall of knowledge and information filtered through our perception of lived experience.

The gift of architecting story.

If the conversation between the two hemispheres of the brain is impeded due to the constriction of the corpus callosum—the part responsible for communication between the two sides—then it puts the viability of cognitive functions and processes on either side in a tough spot.

With communication between the hemispheres challenged, the frontal cortex also becomes constricted and potentially underdeveloped. This becomes a problem when the process of thinking resides in the frontal cortex and is key, for obvious reasons, to learning. The frontal cortex is assigned the responsibility of executive functioning with tasks such as planning, prioritizing, organizing, time management, and more. The strength of our frontal cortex and its executive functioning abilities is key to emotional regulation which is extremely important when we realize that the amygdala, the seat of emotions, becomes exaggerated as a result of trauma.

Working with executive functioning and the learning process is the ability to pay attention, engage memory and language, all things impacted by the injury trauma can cause to the brain.

The synthesis of the research from my studies, and my understanding from the patriarchs that paved the way, led me to what I now refer to it as the *Unintended Consequences of Untended Wounds*. An sample presentation of the continuum follows:

- Trauma occurs in childhood.
- Trauma dysregulates the brain.
- Learning is impeded.
- Maladaptive emotions and behaviors show up in the classroom.
- Students are referred for special needs testing.
- Misdiagnosis occurs.
- Costly, inaccurate treatments and inadequate accommodations follow.
- Trauma intensifies; students become increasingly vulnerable and susceptible to additional maladies and high-risk behaviors.

- Mental health issues begin to occur.
- Service providers and caseloads increase ([a] mental health therapist, [b] social worker/case manager, [c] substance abuse counselor, [d] grief counselor, [e] probation and corrections officer).
- Dependency on government assistance programs and costs escalate.
- Impacts multiply, i.e., Family breakdown, crime rates, incarceration, addiction, suicide, unemployment, and economies.

> **NOTE**: Trauma is not a respecter of socioeconomics. While poverty is reported as one of the number one indicator and is an exacerbator of trauma, affluency can serve as a mitigator and help afford better strategies to hide.

Not only would I find answers for educators and students, but God would use my research to help bring another level of healing in my own journey. This parallel journey of discovery eventually led me to curate what I call the **Blueprint of Trauma's Comprehensive Expression (TCE)** (see Figure 1). TCE provides one presentation at 30,000 ft of the comprehensiveness of trauma's influence. The purpose of the blueprint is to help bring context needed to interpret some of the components, to give a better idea of where and how they might fit, and again, to emphasize a 30,000 ft. view.

When you can have a deeper understanding of the different components and their influence, it positions you to more accurately locate yourself within the larger framework. Of course, within the areas highlighted on the blueprint, there are a myriad of sub-topics that could be explored, but not for this writing, and certainly not all my area of expertise. What is shared is my synthesis, and experience presented in a way that hopefully, as I said, helps to bring understanding.

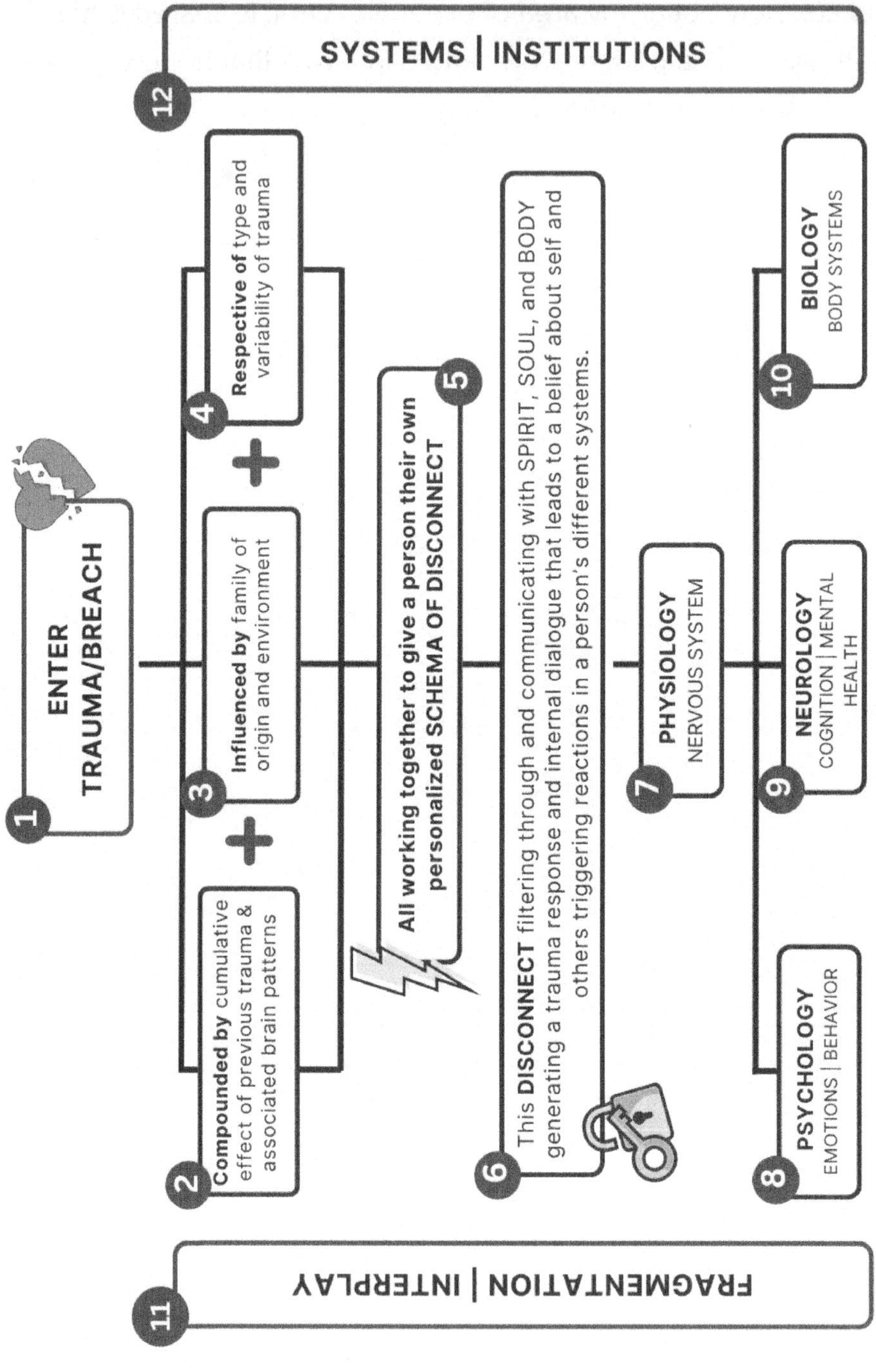


*Figure 1. Blueprint of Trauma's Comprehensive Expression*

## Blueprint of Trauma's Comprehensive Expression

1 - **Enter trauma**

It starts with a disruptive incident that tends to destabilize a person's emotional and psychological equilibrium. We often call it trauma. If you don't like using the word trauma, you may choose another - wound, brokenness, adversity, unfortunate event.

In the work of Dr. Gabor Mate'[2], he defines trauma not as an external event, but of an internal wound resulting from the experience. He talks about, like the blueprint shares, the affect this internal scarring can have on the nervous system, body, and psyche, manifesting in various ways later in life.

Liz Mullinar, a matriarch in the work of trauma from Australia, and founder of Heal for Life[3], defines trauma as a deeply distressing or disturbing experience that can have long-lasting effects on an individual's mental, emotional, and physical well-being. When it occurs in childhood, it impacts the development of the brain affecting how we process and think. Early on, when I was receiving pushback on my "*new thought*" regarding the correlation between misdiagnosis and trauma, Liz was the one that validated my hypothesis.

2 - **Compounded by cumulative effect of previous trauma and associated brain patterns**

In the book, *It Didn't Start with You*, Mark Wolynn explores the concept of inherited family trauma and its impact on an individual's life. I call this the "*before zero stuff*". Wolynn argues that the unresolved traumas of our ancestors can deeply influence

2 Maté, G. (2011). *When the body says no: The cost of hidden stress*. Vintage Canada.
3 https://healforlife.com.au/

our emotional and behavioral patterns, often in subtle and unconscious ways. These unconscious ways directly related to pre-existing neural pathways formed in utero influencing how we receive, perceive and respond to those things outside the womb.

Whether we are talking about the "*before zero stuff*" or additional traumatic events in early life, the results are cumulative causing compounding effects.

3 - **Influenced by family of origin and environment.**
You can't over emphasize the importance of secure attachments and emotional nurturance for children's healthy neurobiological brain development, particularly highlighting the critical period before the age of three. The home environment and the healthy or unhealthy attachments provided there impact early relational dynamics that further shape trauma responses and their respective coping mechanisms.

Attachment is like your trauma insurance. Attachment represents relationship and **relationship is a forerunner for everything**. In the research, four attachment types are typically discussed:

1. Healthy (dependable, consistent, comforting, supportive),
2. Avoidant (too much to deal with, I just won't think about it, emotionally unavailable),
3. Ambivalent (may be OK now, but not tomorrow, unpredictable, not reliable), and
4. Disorganized (not sure which end is up, sometimes comforting, sometimes a source of fear).

Everyone is hoping for insurance policy #1, but much of the time many of us end up with one of the others. Sometimes life circumstances will try to bundle but, for the most part, one type presents itself most prominent. In my story, the prominent attachment type was avoidance.

My entry into the world began in the deep South and consisted of a very conservative upbringing. My father was the pastor of a mainstream denomination. He didn't know about the "*before zero stuff*". He didn't understand that the fact that he was raised by an alcoholic father could have any influence or bearing on him. He made a choice to not drink alcohol and that was the end of it, or was it? As trauma bonding would have it, you guessed it, my mother was also raised by an alcoholic father. My grandfathers both ended up dying because of their addiction, and within two weeks of each other; add to the mix, death of siblings at a young age. This Niagara of cortisol drenched their foundations, while broken congregants—pretending to be whole—struggled under rules they didn't understand or believe, but dared not question.

This was the environment within which I would experience sexual abuse at the hand of my uncle at an early age, you can only imagine how that went. This paved the way for other compounding events and would create the perfect storm for what would follow in later years.

Unfortunately, what occurs is that after generations of the "*before zero stuff*", it can end up having an impact on life outside the womb. It can impact every part of our person. Beyond my current comprehension and understanding, it doesn't necessarily decide to show up day one. It could spring up 10 years down the road.

With all that said, after you arrive in family, the hope is that you show up in an environment with emotionally healthy adults who can help you process and heal. In an ideal environment, the parents and caregivers would be in pursuit of their own growth and healing. As inferred by my own story, this is not always the case. Although I believe most parents are doing the best they can. Parents, including my parents, and including myself, often find themselves living out of their own unhealed and unresolved woundings.

Dr. Mate' would tell you there is no need to blame your parents; it didn't start with them either. Being a parent that really screwed up at times, dishing out my share of trauma – just ask my children – this provides a little solace.

4 - **Respective of type and variability of trauma**
Next on our blueprint is consideration for the different types and variabilities within trauma. This means I could have had the same thing happen to me that happened to you, and based on the myriad of variables and their interplay, the outward expression will present differently:

- Where did it begin?
- When did it begin?
- How old were you when it began?
- Where were you living when it began?
- What was the environment like you were living in when it began?

The answer to these questions influences the individuality of trauma's impact. These expressions are unique personal and situational factors shaping the trauma experience and the ones listed above are just a few. The cultural and geographic implications on the interplay are significant to understand as well.

5 - All working together to give a person their own personalized **SCHEMA OF DISCONNECT.**
These personal expressions coupled with the influence from patterns created from the "*before zero stuff*", the attachment styles found in the origin environment, all work together to produce an individualized schema of disconnect in your stress response system.

6 - Your personal brand of **DiSCONNECT** filters through and communicates with **SPIRIT, SOUL, and BODY** generating a trauma response and internal dialogue that leads to a belief about self and others. The stress response system driven by the internal dialogue.

Due to our stress response system, and our fear-based need to "run for cover", our processing can become fragmented. Much of the time, our exaggerated emotions and the impeding behaviors they cause skew or confuse our ability to see and perceive clearly. An internal dialogue ensues that seems to never shut off. And sometimes, you may not even be able to articulate the feeling or thought. Some of the dialogue may sound like *what did I do to deserve this? I must be the problem. Something must be wrong with me. I am not worthy to be regarded or protected* and the list goes on. That last one was mine. Certainly, that had to be the truth, if, in my young mind, my dad was not willing to confront his brother about molesting his own daughter. What else are you to conclude? These self-accusations acting as a source of energy to these rapid-fire synapses going off continually in the brain. If you do not have caring, and emotionally stable adults there to listen, validate, help you process and heal, then you begin growing in the direction of the wound.

## The worst thing about childhood trauma is not the actual event, but the lie about ourselves that we believe because of it.

The impact of the presenting trauma with all its interplays enters in through our central nervous system which then sends signals and messages out across other interconnected systems. Our human body and the systems contained therein represent a network of signals (frequencies). When those signals are interrupted by trauma, of any kind, misfiring signals to the different systems to which they are assigned become interrupted and hindered. We could say our signals get crossed or become scrambled. Using the concept of "*signals being crossed*", when this happens in the brain it creates disruption or miscommunication between neurons and different brain regions. This miscommunication can lead to confusion, inefficiency, or even malfunctions.

Simultaneously, strapped with the wrong accusations about self, and the feelings of disconnection, our emotions continue to wreak havoc. The source or origin emotions inviting other emotions to come join. Think interplay. Can you hear it? Shame calls out to self-rejection and self-rejection gladly accommodates. After all, they do say misery loves company. However, if shame and self-rejection are left to themselves, it will not be long before despair comes knocking at the door leaving us looking for ways to shut off the noise.

Over time, when not addressed, these maladaptive emotions lead to bigger issues; issues like anxiety, depression, dissociation, and more - eventually progressing into mental health challenges – and all the while unresolved trauma providing the building blocks.

**While our emotions are having a hate fest – whether turned inwardly or outwardly - the discontent and dissonance in our psyche is creating disease in our mind and body.**

I was in my 40's before I had the realization that every decision and choice I had ever made came from the place of believing a lie about myself. I had spent all my time, to that point, attempting – as I mitigated, coped, and self-protected along the way – to understand who I was, and although I could put a label on something or had a category to fit it in, I still had a difficult time finding myself in the context of the story.

The aha! moment happened on the couch of a psychologist I had went to visit. *I was about to say counselor because that sounds better.* Through a process of unpacking and sharing, I came to learn that the who that I thought I was, was only a persona I had created to manage and cope with all the things; all the things that (1) I didn't understand, or (2) I didn't want to understand for fear of what I would learn. As I journeyed through the doctoral program, it would become even clearer.

When I enrolled in the doctoral program, I knew in my knower I was to pursue the doctorate, but I did not entirely understand the why. I had pressed through the rigor of seven years of doctoral studies and counted among the less than 50% of the cohort that completed the degree. The academic rigor was not for the faint of heart. On any given occasion you could find me cussing, crying, or speaking in an unknown tongue, and let's not forget the persistent gut issues.

## The Lost Child Theory

When we are not truly present in the moment, our stories remain locked inside.

After 7 long years, it finally became clear. Mercy found me in a hotel room on Virginia Beach. It was as if I finally found what I was looking for. It was as if the research lifted off the page. I called it *The Lost Child Theory*. (I know others have used similar terminology.) *The Lost Child Theory* states that when someone experiences trauma in childhood – while they are in the midst of developing in every way – their first response is to find safety, they run for cover, disconnecting from their truest essence. Essence hijacked; they are robbed of the experience of NOW. They find it difficult to be where they are, to be present. When this happens three critical attributes needed for healthy wellbeing and flourishing are displaced or *lost*: Lost Support, Lost Script, and Lost Sense of Self.

**Lost Support** is where the healthy attachments needed with caring adults become disorganized causing distrust and feelings of fear, even if only perceived. This is most impactful for those that didn't receive policy #1 *of the trauma insurance*.

**Lost Script** scaffolds on top of the feeling of displacement skewing a person's life narrative. A life narrative is what helps a person put a frame around life. Then, suddenly in a moment of time, the frame is gone, snatched away. Life doesn't make sense. Why would a grown man think it was a good idea to violate a young girl or boy to satisfy his own unmet and maladaptive needs? Note, that this vertigo of reality influences everything we understand about cause and effect, not to mention the universal distrust it creates. Lost Support and Lost Script work together to set the stage for the third of the lost attributes, Lost Sense of Self.

**Lost Sense of Self** is our understanding of self required to exercise personal agency. Not only are we unable to make sense of the world around us, but we do not have the first idea where to begin to find our place in it. We may have an *identifier*, but we don't know where we fit in the story.

After completing the doctoral process, I indeed had found some answers for students – granted it took me 7 plus years – but I had also found answers for myself. **I was the lost child**.

Feeling good about this huge accomplishment, I was ready to tell everyone what I knew. The first assignment, in my mind, was to create a course for educators. I saw them as the first responders in the classroom, and they needed to know so they could quit making errant referrals. It made sense to me, anyway. However, I quickly realized, the political current was much stronger than

I. Albeit my pure heart and good intentions, teachers were not in a place ready to receive, through no fault of their own. My observations were and I was told by many teachers that their autonomy had been stripped, and many had their creativity replaced with a script.

Although there were symptoms and challenges that needed addressing in the classroom, the root cause was systemic. **For generations, we have built brokenness into the system, which means the only thing it can do, is the thing that it was made to do; exacerbate and perpetuate the brokenness.**

Not to pick on my childhood, or those that were charged with its nurturing, but because of my mother's upbringing, compounded with the pressures of being a pastor's wife, she learned to disconnect and deny. There were just some things that you did not talk about. Ever. Living in a land of *pretty is as pretty does-speak only when spoken to-quit crying or I will give you something to cry about,* my mother responded as most would and shut her emotions down or at least did a wonderful job of suppressing them, calling it all good. She built brokenness into her system. If situations got intense, and they did, the response was *it happened, there is nothing we can do about it, move on.* This kind of response is an indicator of living in an avoidant type of environment. When I experienced my own childhood trauma, this was the environment, and I responded in kind. I learned to restrict and suppress my emotions. I think we all understand, even if in theory, that pressing through to deny the truth or reality of a thing is not true resilience, it is normalized dysfunction, and we have become masters.

We have normalized dysfunction to the widening of the breach and as a result increasing the gravitational pull of the infraction on our wellbeing. Years of normalizing generational, historical, and traumatic narratives have left individuals, families, and communities desensitized, broken, and settling for less.

Can you imagine having the title of Director of Equity in Education, for example, and finding it hard to show up every day to work, because you are not buying what is being sold? However, you keep showing up, ignoring and even betraying what is screaming on the inside of you, because, well, you need the job. **I know those people**. The betrayal of self competing with a louder voice that tells you that you must do to be and to be accepted, you must perform. **I know that voice**.

**Oh, the injustice that the caterpillar would never become the butterfly. Essence denied by others is one thing, but essence denied by self—that's a whole other thing: that's the worst betrayal of all.**

**This is a universal problem**. Billions of children are affected, many of them now walking around in grown up bodies. Let's continue with the blueprint.

7 - **Physiology**
Continuing to normalize dysfunction, willfully choosing to disregard self, and accepting it as so, causes our stress response system to idle on high.

When we are caught in the day-to-day fragmentation and incongruence that is the result of compounding chaotic and hypervigilant effects of unaddressed trauma, we find ourselves stuck in survival mode. Instead of being able to see the big picture, we get stuck in the individual moments of crisis. Not only are we stuck in survival mode, but these rapid-fire messages are looping through our nervous system and brain playing heck on our psychology (mental wellbeing), neurology (cognition), and biology (physical bodies).

8 - **Psychology**

To recap, trauma that occurs in childhood creates dysregulation in the brain – cognitively and emotionally. This dysregulation in the brain impedes learning and as a result maladaptive emotions and behaviors show up in our lives, and for the purpose of this writing, in the classroom. This has already been stated, and will be stated again. In response, errant student referrals are made for special needs testing leading to misinterpretation, misrepresentation, and misdiagnosis – serving as a key contributor to mental health challenges.

9 - **Neurology**

Compounded by the psychological impact that keep children in a vigilant state, frequently disassociating (checking out) or self-protecting (checking you out), the cognitive processes required for learning are also negatively impacted. This influence delays development and interrupts academic progress.

Bonnie Brandes, pioneer in primitive reflexes[4], and reflex integration, states, "*Many do not realize that neurological connections called primitive reflexes are responsible for almost*

---

4 Brandes, B. *The Symphony of Primitive Reflexes*. www.reflexintegration.net

*everything we do from speech to cognition to movement. They also affect every aspect of learning and school success."*

We referenced earlier the compounding effects of cumulative trauma, in the same way, the physiology, psychology, and neurology work together to put a burden on your biology resulting in disease.

10 - **Biology**
The unresolved trauma that keeps the stress response system in high alert causes interruption in neurodevelopment. This produces the chronic elevation of stress hormones, increasing anxiety, interrupting sleep, suppressing the immune system, and creating inflammation leading to disease.

For example, why would we be surprised when a population of people historically marginalized, sold the generational lie of less-than, living with a stress response system idling in high alert, show up statistically having a higher-than-normal blood pressure or heart disease rates.

Imagine feeling that everything you said and did was being judged, that was me. On top of that, I happen to have a strong Southern accent. Then, God gives me a message to help heal and free others and expose injustice. In the past I have felt paralyzed when I would think about sharing out anything. One of the physical manifestations of this was a "diagnosis" of diverticulitis. Attempting to store things on the inside - for fear of being judged - that need to be on the outside can create literal inflammation in your body, and in my case, my intestines.

As stated, this is a 30,000 ft. view. There are those experts in the different areas mentioned, my intent is to connect the bigger pieces under one conversation to help move us closer to clarity. We now have the resources and research available to help us make these connections. The point is about making the connection so we can heal, not so we stay in a place of victimhood or vulnerability to victimization. This underscores the need to understand the next spot on the blueprint.

Trauma's "F" word and the antithesis of ordered and synergistic flow.

11 - **Fragmentation and interplay**

We are spirit, we are soul, and we are body. The disconnection from essence of true self —away from our spirit—at the point of a trauma, creates a hunger and desire to find purpose and meaning or simply put, get reconnected. Now, fighting to find our way back, requires navigating the path crowded and impeded by the interplay of your personalized SCHEMA OF DISCONNECT.

**NOTE**: The blueprint was meant to provide context and understanding, but it is important to point out there are other contributors and exacerbating influences like digital (social media, video games), environmental, and chemical.

If you are someone who has the tendency to operate out of that place of survival and pressing through, remember again, the point of acknowledgement of the event and pain is to process and heal not to stay in the place of wounding. Rather, find the new space (the resources and support) of true resilience and contribution.

We don't want to stay in the place of fear and wrong beliefs about ourselves or about others. We don't want to continue living out of a false persona in hopes of fitting in. We don't want to turn a blind eye and or stick our fingers in our ears negatively impacting our minds and bodies. **The ongoing cost of living contrary to self has become unsustainable, as individuals and as a society.** We must make a choice to no longer abdicate the stewardship of our own hearts and minds to another, not another person, not another system.

It is time for us to take personal responsibility to do the due diligence to steward the health and wellbeing of our lives and the lives of our children. When we decide to partner with personal healing and the pursuit of true essence, we can begin to see clearer, what seems so overwhelming. When we choose personal healing, we can begin to lift our head up to see a **wider view**. Life is no longer a big selfie. With a wider view and perspective, we are better able to identify patterns and connect the dots.

12 - **Systems and Institutions**

As we begin to understand and address the impact trauma has personally, we begin to see the multiplied effect on systems and society. In the next chapter, we will discuss the mass effect on systems when societies fail to heal.

# CHAPTER ONE – THE PROBLEM–MICRO

*Disconnect from Essence*

> "The who that I thought I was, was only a persona
> I had created to manage and cope."
> — Dr. Ivy Bonk

### *Integrating the Reset*

1. How does this chapter redefine or deepen your understanding of the causes of learning and behavioral challenges in students?

2. What do you think are the dangers of ignoring trauma in educational settings?

3. How does this model expand your awareness of how trauma expresses itself across the whole of a person?

4. What's one thing you feel called to *change, explore, or heal* after reading this chapter?

5. What are some ways that you, as part of a group, community, or team, can begin to create space for authentic healing, identity reclamation, and systemic reimagination?

# CHAPTER TWO
# THE PROBLEM—MACRO

In Chapter Two, I widen the lens from personal trauma to societal impact, showing how unresolved trauma on a mass scale destabilizes our systems, starting with education. I share how misdiagnosis, misdirected discipline, and deep inequities are not isolated issues, but symptoms of a system that has normalized dysfunction. The statistics around poverty, incarceration, and special education disparities point to a deeper, trauma-unaware design. I contend that education, as the predecessor system, must be reset at the root. True healing demands we dismantle broken systems, confront historical inequities, and rebuild for coherence. Without this, we risk reproducing harm across future generations.

# CHAPTER TWO
# THE PROBLEM — MACRO

We have briefly discussed the course trauma can take as it impacts the life of a person. But what happens when that impact is multiplied by millions and then those millions are placed within a system. In Figure 1, Blueprint of Trauma's Comprehensive Expression, there is the label SYSTEMS and INSTITUTIONS. Systems and institutions are how the FRAGMENTATION and INTERPLAY are leveraged and perpetuated.

Power brokers (*broken boys and girls in grown up bodies positioned in places of authority struggling to find their sense of self by controlling and manipulating outcomes*) have spent decades promoting learned helplessness, dependency, and control, while manipulating systems, data, research, and people, to maintain the same. However, we have now reached the point where the weight of our own making overtakes the ability of the fractured structure we have created to support it.

*Figure 2. A Case for Education's Reset*

The fallout and incalculable cost are on mass display. In our society, we live in an ecosystem of systems. In this societal ecosystem, the education system goes first. It is the predecessor.

Here is what we know. With few exceptions, the commonality between persons who have experienced childhood trauma with impact lingering into adulthood is that they have all crossed over the bridge of education.[5] The following shows the continuum of how unresolved trauma is filtered through the ecosystem of systems, with a sampling of outcomes and related costs.

## One Thing Leads to Another

**Education**. It goes something like this, traumatized parent/caregiver sends traumatized child and their dysregulated brain off to school with other traumatized students to attempt to engage, in many cases, an agenda-driven curriculum that has no relevance or for which the child has no context, delivered in fragmented and incongruent ways by leaders and educators with their own unaddressed and unresolved trauma.

In a system charged to nurture and foster growth and development in children, this should be viewed as unacceptable. Schools should be emotionally safe environments where children are honored and where attachment and relationships with the adults in their lives are encouraged with space for this to grow and heal.

---

5 Bonk, I. (2019, July 31). *Interrupting the cycle of inequity in education* [Conference presentation]. 3rd Annual Philadelphia Trauma Conference, Philadelphia, PA, United States.

Emotional safety is formed in secure connections with a baseline of unconditional worth. It is a non-negotiable if we expect children to develop and mature. This baseline of unconditional worth countering the lie of trauma that tells a person "*You are not worth it*".[6]

If the mass fragmentation goes unchecked, environments will remain unsafe, students and families will not receive the services promised, and the educators will continue to be frustrated, overworked, and unfulfilled. The misinterpretation, misrepresentation, and misdiagnosis —yes, I said it again—from the unresolved trauma only serving to perpetuate the brokenness and increase the pressure of the toxic stress that it creates.

In education, this leads to:

(1) Incentivization toward low performance,
(2) Rise in special education and affiliated cost,
(3) Increase in high school dropouts, and/or
(4) Continued surge of graduates leaving what was supposed to be education in much need of academic remediation.

The reality is ugly. Here's one. If literacy is supposed to be an economic determinant, then someone will need to explain how after 40 years of investing trillions of dollars, it is reported that 50% of the population cannot even read at a 6th grade level[7]. Some things don't make sense because they just don't make sense.

6 Maté, G. (2022). *The myth of normal: Trauma, illness, and healing in a toxic culture*. Penguin.

7 Hanson, Melanie. "U.S. Public Education Spending Statistics" EducationData.org, February 8, 2025, https://educationdata.org/public-education-spending-statistics

Students in public education,, typically from the age of 5 until they are 18, spend more waking hours in school and school related activities than they do anywhere else. This is the same age range where they experience much of their development leading to adulthood. This makes the environment at the school extremely important.

We have already established that students need adults in their lives, both at home and at school, who are dependable, consistent, and predictable. If childhood trauma unaddressed and unresolved lingers into adulthood, then we shouldn't be surprised when family members, school leaders, classroom teachers, resource officers, and staff are triggered by students, as students are reflecting the dissonance and lack of attunement inside the adult. Unfortunately, it too often appears that the convergence of massive amounts of unresolved trauma in society has left adults acting more like children while expecting children to act like adults.

School climates filled with the reactionary and punitive responses by school staff due to the intersect of their own intolerances with the undesirable or maladaptive emotions and behaviors lead to unnecessary outcomes. Beyond the impact on the emotional and mental wellbeing of students, this type of environment effects academic achievement, classroom management, safety, and more.

As mentioned, child maltreatment results in the impairment of cognitive functioning. This includes associated externalizing and internalizing behaviors. As pointed out in the blueprint, these adaptive responses from trauma coupled with insecure attachment in the home environment creates an internal battle of emotions, among them anxiety, fear, shame, and incompetence. The affective, behavioral, and cognitive influences then show up in the classroom with educators, leaders, and staff unable to discern, due to the interference, in part, by their own unresolved trauma.

Lack of support, limited resources, fragmented and incongruent processes, with students that are in heightened states weigh an educator down. The effects of misalignment, fragmentation, overload, result in their working at reduced capacity, all while exerting 150% of their available energy.

In one school project I participated in, the teacher was asked to complete an observation of her students using a supplemental tool from The Neurosequential Network (www.neurosequential.com) referred to as the NME Mini-Map. Using a scale of 1 to 4, the tool provides, by way of educator observation, a snapshot of the brain's mediated strengths and weaknesses in relation to peers in their same grade. In the area of Communication/Language Skills, the teacher ranked every student as a "1". One (1) means "*needs significant improvement/serious challenges*". As I reviewed the feedback, I thought it highly unlikely that all these students were impaired in this region of the brain. Rather, as pointed out, this was more likely an example of an ability not yet developed. If you live in a stressful home environment and not allowed to exercise your voice or your voice is not heard or valued, your expressive language skills will become underdeveloped and will become even more so with added exacerbators, i.e., excessive screen time. **This does not mean that skill cannot be developed. It only means that it has not been given the opportunity to be developed.** If the educator is not equipped, supported, and is working at a reduced capacity, we can anticipate one of two responses, or a combination of the two:

(1) A referral for special needs testing, and/or
(2) A behavioral referral for disciplinary actions.

(1) **Special Needs Testing I Misdiagnosis.** The existing methods and practices within education is to refer students exhibiting maladaptive emotions and behaviors for learning disabilities and special needs testing. Unfortunately, many of these same symptoms are common among traumatized students. In the public education system, if a child is academically lagging - up until the point of a predetermined age threshold - they are considered developmentally delayed. Once they reach that age threshold, to receive services, they must be "*identified*". They go from being considered developmentally delayed to intellectually or emotionally disabled. It is at this intersect that we find what I refer to as the *trap door*. The trap door is when a decision regarding a student's cognitive ability is made at a time when their brain is malleable and still in development producing errant outcomes. Dr. Bruce Perry[8] shares that learning is a state dependent activity. If you have a student in a heightened state and you are going to take a snapshot in time by way of an assessment to determine whether they are learning disabled or have special needs, you can be relatively certain the feedback you will receive will not be accurate. It may provide you with data and inform, to a degree, the situation at hand, but clearly not the information

8 www.neurosequential.com

needed to make a decision that can lead to life-altering results. I mean, who wants to receive a diagnosis of lung cancer when you merely have bronchitis?

These errant outcomes not only impact the student's perception of self, but the perception of others toward them. This is an example of how we have created a system or process within a system where we benefit from the brokenness of another, making a disadvantage an advantage. I know it sounds harsh when you say it. Even now, attempting to find the words to explicitly communicate makes me very sad. It seems incomprehensible how this could even be the case.

The reality is that for many, and I would dare say most — as has already been stated but deserves repeating— the likelihood is that the children are not truly learning disabled, but rather their true learning ability has been masked by maladaptive emotions and behaviors hiding or deflecting from their true gifting and abilities. It's what I call the *Dr. Trajecklyl and Mr. Hide Effect™* of trauma. When this is not discerned or addressed within the education system, it can only result in a life lived well below potential, at best.

(2) **Disciplinary Action | Punitive Responses**. As shared, the emotional and relational deficits created by trauma cause persons to mitigate and cope by engaging in high-risk behaviors. When undesired emotions and behaviors show up in the classroom, they are met with disciplinary practices that lead to referrals to resource officers or school climate

> staff. This continues to reinforce negative messaging. Feeling hurt and now angry from disrespect and devaluing, the child continues to exhibit undesirable behaviors that lead to the continued and escalated engagement with resource officers and discipline staff resulting in punitive measures being enforced. The perpetuation of misrepresentation has the potential to turn hurt and anger into rage and violence often misdirected toward others.

When we invest in the types of programs built on fear and punitive measures, rather than trust and relationship-building, we are making value statements, and not only about the students. Criminalizing behaviors due to maladaptive emotions from trauma communicates an anticipation of wrongdoing, instead of an expectation of good.

We must have schools that create safe and supportive learning environments and that address the root causes of perceived disciplinary issues without our first response being a punitive one. We must shift to alternative approaches and practices that can be implemented to address in restorative ways.

As mentioned, symptoms associated with trauma such as those mentioned including mood fluctuations, hypervigilance, dissociation, difficulty managing behavior, impulsivity, and more can often be misidentified as indicators of learning disabilities or deviant behaviors. Mislabeling and the wrong application of strategies and interventions from misrepresentation and misdiagnosis, whether a misinterpretation of a cognitive ability or a punitive response to a student's emotions and behaviors, is further traumatizing. This opens students up to other maladies and misfortunes leading to, in many cases, mental health challenges. Coming to school each day should not look and sound like a shake-down at the airport by an angry TSA agent. I **have witnessed this.**

**Risk of Mental Health Concerns**. According to NAMI (National Alliance on Mental Health), over 50% of the mental health issues are diagnosed by the time a person is 14 years of age.[9] Really? The gross and blatant incongruency of this statistic with the preciousness of human life should make us sick to our stomach.

We can no longer stand idly by while high school dropouts continue to increase, drug addiction continues to escalate, violence on our city streets soar, mental health skyrockets, challenges within workforce continue to rise, and prisons hang out "*at capacity*" signs and ask ourselves why. We know why.

Based on my experience and observation, it is my opinion, that it is premature, unjust, and inequitable — when due diligence to address these challenges from within education have not been exhausted — to identify a student suspected of trauma of possessing a learning disability, a deviant behavior, or a mental health disorder. Rather, **our first response is to consider this a capacity issue in time discerned through the lens of trauma**.

The continued reliance on ineffective school processes—despite their proven harm—exposes a fragmented, siloed system that prioritizes dysfunction over student well-being. We must see how this feeds systemic inequities, beginning in education and affecting every system thereafter.

---

9 https://www.nami.org/kids-teens-and-young-adults/kids-and-parents/

Dr. Stuart Ablon of Think:Kids, Massachusetts General Hospital, often shares a quote he learned from his grandfather,

**"If you call a dog by a name long enough, they will answer to it."**

Remember, students respond to the adults around them. If they are met with expectations of wrongdoing and failure, they will most likely rise to the occasion. The same is true when you choose to believe the best.

Following is a snapshot of the influence on other systems (not intended to be inclusive or complete):

**Health (Mental/Physical).** Restating what we already discussed, the unresolve of trauma leads to poor health outcomes, both mentally and physically.

Often mental health challenges can be perpetuated by misdiagnosis. If you are diagnosed with something you do not in fact have, this only serves to worsen the problem and acts as gateway to high-risk behaviors like substance abuse, addiction, sex trafficking, suicide, and other maladies.

**Workforce.** This tapped down potential from being undereducated not only creates the need for remedial education but causes difficulty for those integrating into the workplace. It produces the outcomes of underemployment, and unemployment, not to mention the cost from lack of performance, lost productivity, attrition rates, and waste of training dollars.

**Social Services (Welfare/Foster Care).** The sense of overwhelm and failure that are the residuals of unaddressed woundings sets a person up to be the perfect candidate for systemic dependency and chronic poverty, thus continuing the cycle. Families overrun with the stress of all things listed above, find they cannot adequately provide the resources necessary to address fundamental issues. The stress of it all progressing into mental health challenges further leads families and children into resource inadequacies and more trauma. It is not surprising that when a person feels overly stressed and not knowing what to do in any given situation that they might respond in an unhealthy and harmful way toward self or others. Unfortunately, this scenario can cause an outside agency to come in and remove a child from its home, which compounds the trauma not address it or find themselves suddenly involved in the criminal justice system.

**Criminal Justice,**

According to the National Council on Disabilities (NCD, 2015), 85% of incarcerated youth are reported to have learning disabilities compared to 11-12% of a typical school population. If you are reading this, that statistic should be alarming and unsettling. I assert, as established earlier, that most of these young people are not truly learning disabled rather their measured capacity at a particular age threshold was interpreted as a permanent ability.

Subsequently, and not surprisingly, black and brown students are suspended and expelled at a rate three times greater than white students (U.S. Department of Education, 2014). The passing of additional crime bills put in place years ago assures that the school-to-prison pipeline will arrive at its final stop of mass incarceration.

## Let the Numbers Do the Talking

The following is a sample of statistics and costs from a variety of sources highlighting the impact on the systemic continuum:

**Statistics**

- 11 million children live in poverty, including 1 in 7 children of color, and 1 in 6 under the age of 5 (The State of America's Children, 2023).
- Child Protective Services (CPS) reported over 3 million investigations for child neglect or abuse (CPS, 2021).
- Black children are five times as likely as white children to attend schools that are highly segregated by race and ethnicity – 69.2% to 12.9% (Garcia, 2020).
- Black children are more than twice as likely as white children to attend high-poverty schools - 72.4% to 31.3% (Garcia, 2020).
- Black students are more likely to be identified for special education than their White peers (Grindal et al., 2020).
- Black students are suspended and expelled at a rate three times greater than white students. On average, 5% of white students are suspended, compared to 16% of black students (U.S. Department of Education, 2014).
- While black students represent 16% of student enrollment, they represent 27% of students referred to law enforcement and 31% of students subjected to a school-related arrest

(U.S. Department of Education, 2014).

- Black youth nationwide are more than four times as likely to be detained or committed to a juvenile facility as their white peers (The Sentencing Project, 2019).
- Forty-one percent of youth incarcerated are Black, even though Black Americans comprise only 15% of all youth across the United States (The Sentencing Project, 2019).
- There are more than two million juvenile referrals to police from schools each year (Southern Coalition for Social Justice, 2014).
- Despite only accounting for 6% of the general population, African American males represent nearly 50% of the prison population (Perry & Bright, 2012).

**Costs**

| Topic | Source | Cost |
|---|---|---|
| Childhood Trauma/Abuse | Prevent Child Abuse | $220 million every day/$80 billion (National) |
| Special Education | EdSource | $13 billion/annually (National) |
| Remedial Education | Inside Higher Ed | $1.3 billion/annually (National) |
| Child Welfare | Congressional Research Service | $11.7 billion/annually (National) |
| Mental Health | CNBC | $225 billion/annually (National) |
| Suicide | Rural Health Information | $70 billion/annually (National) |

| | | |
|---|---|---|
| Substance Abuse | Georgetown University's Health Policy Institute | $532 billion/annually (National) |
| Criminal Justice | Vera Institute | $295 billion/annually (National) |
| Juvenile Justice | Office of Juvenile Justice and Delinquency Prevention | $344 million/annually (National) |

*Table 1. Sampling of related costs*

## The Journey from There to Here

**"The root cause of all the problems we have in the world today is ignorance of course." Maya Angelou**

My interpretation of this quote, in the absence of punctuation, is through the lens or in the context of problem solving. *Of course*, ignorance is a problem, but more specifically, not understanding the course you have taken to get to where you are (we are) is the real issue. **Understanding the root is top priority, the first consideration, when creating a solve**. Resetting equitable foundations in education is an exercise of deconstruction. It involves the process of dismantling structures that are not serving the outcomes of flourishing while at the same time reclaiming and repurposing those things that should remain. It is critical to understand what is being removed, and why, and how we got here in the first place, *lest it* and *we return*.

Implementing a systemic solution to societal inequities requires understanding other complex and interrelated issues that have contributed to its existence. I mention a few.

**Enslavement**. Although slavery is reported to have ended in 1865, policies and legislation continued to remain in place that bore and continues to bear the marks of enslavement, disenfranchisement, and prejudice.

In a quote from Woodrow Wilson in 1909, then President of Princeton University, he addressed the New York City School Teacher's Association:

> *"We want one class of persons to have a liberal education, and we want another class, a very much larger class, of every society, to forgo the privileges of a liberal education and fit themselves to perform specific difficult manual tasks."*[10]

Imagine yourself a person still fighting for freedom hearing these comments. It would sound to me a little too close to the situation I was trying to leave. If disregarding life, assaulting dignity, and blunting potential wasn't enough, we saw the calculated dismantling of the family unit.

**The Fatherless Experiment.** Have you ever heard of the Fatherless Experiment? Maybe not. That's what I call what was occurring between the 1930's and the 1980's. The fatherless

---

10 Doidge, N. (2007). *The brain that changes itself: Stories of personal triumph from the frontiers of brain science*. Penguin.

experiment was a policy that became known as the "*no man in the house*" rule. The "*no man in the house*" rule was an eligibility requirement for obtaining public housing and was a program under the Aid for Families with Dependent Children (AFDC). I am not sure who they were aiding but it was not families and children. The policy was put in place as a part of the Social Security Act of 1935 (www.ssa.gov/history) and was not fully repealed until the 1980's. This intentional and documented assault on the family span fifty years. In 1974, the movie *Claudine*[11], starring Diahanne Carroll and James Earl Jones, highlighted the "*no man in the house*" rule. The movie was billed as a romantic comedy, but after watching I found little funny about it. I saw it more as a veiled attempt at making light of and normalizing brokenness. In case you didn't know, humor is an adaptive coping strategy that can help reduce the burden of a stressful situation. **I know that strategy**, maybe you do too.

**The American Dream**. On the heels of the promises of freedom, and housing, was the aspiration to prosper as people pursued the American Dream. They would call it the War on Poverty. Now, 60 plus years in on this pursuit, and it has turned out to be quite the opposite. It feels more like the war on prosperity. Martin Luther King wasn't killed because he wanted people of different races to gather for a prayer meeting. No, he believed he was created equal which meant just that. If you could prosper, so could he.

Let's be clear. Government programs do not equate to social justice. Increased government dependency is the opposite of that. What was meant as a short-term transition turns into a life

11 https://www.imdb.com/title/tt0071334/

altering enablement. As an example, the small rural town where the demographics have earned this town the recognition as the "poorest" zip code in their state for ten years running (along with a few other deficit recognitions), we find that the minorities make up the majority. The majority minority being the same group most closely aligned with the designation of poor. The residents of this community, in large part, have been taught and have learned well to accept this as their way of being. In this zip code, developers can't secure land quick enough to put up their next low-income housing development. The external activities and the orchestrated cooperation it takes to ensure this stays in place are beyond preposterous. But even more so, the internal searing of consciousness (soul) by the recipients to allow and accept it is heartbreaking.

**If you can't beat them, join them, or just escape by numbing your pain and frustration**. Some writings attribute the beginning of the school-to-prison pipeline to the intersect of the War on Drugs during former President Richard Nixon's administration and the zero-tolerance policies put in place by former President Ronald Reagan. Since the inception of the War on Drugs, like its comrade the War on Poverty, problems have only worsened. When you look at these snapshots, you can begin to understand some things, and you don't have to wonder how or why we have a generational issue in the prison system with black youth and their fathers. This is not an inherent problem due to the color of someone's skin. The idea of such a thing is ridiculous. This, in fact, is a result of an intentional and carefully orchestrated timeline of events.

When did we decide it was acceptable to trade one's brokenness for another's benefit or worse yet convince someone they could benefit from staying broke? Given what has been shared thus far, it is easy to see how the root of compounding and often conflicting circumstances in a person's life intersects with the complex issues of a government system, in this case, education.

These despairing conditions working together to produce a never-ending supply of symptoms. These symptoms only serving the purpose of reproducing the same. It's the proverbial hamster wheel that has been created and must be maintained to fuel the inequity. To receive funding for broken, broken is required. This hamster wheel wastes countless hours of time and energy, unfathomable amounts of monies, and worst of all, the exploitation of millions of lives.

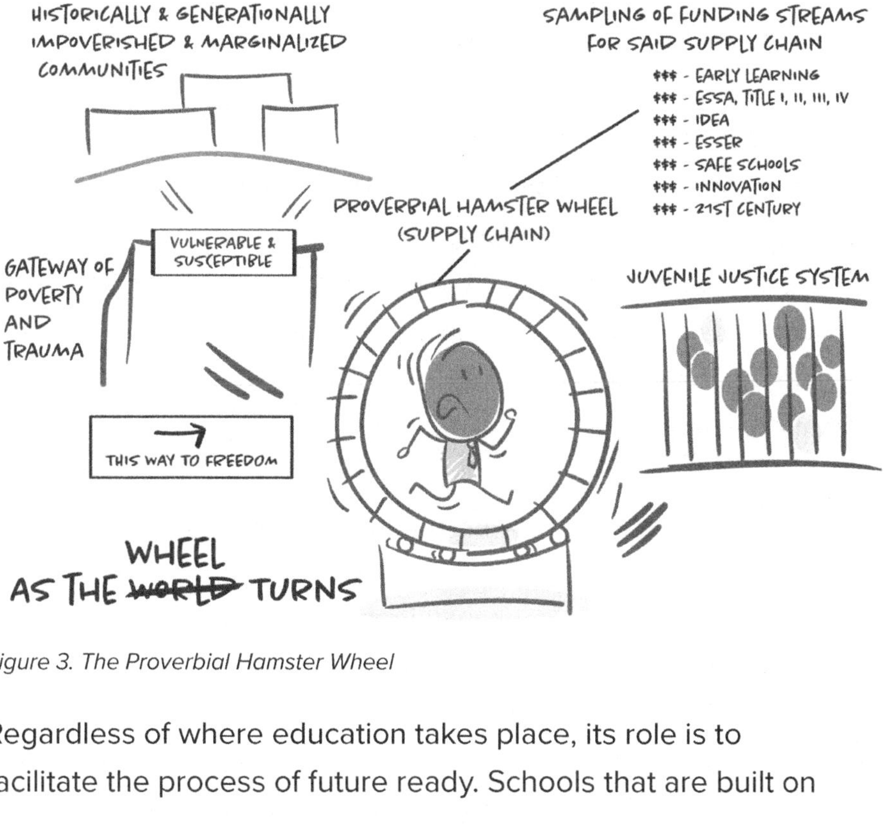


*Figure 3. The Proverbial Hamster Wheel*

Regardless of where education takes place, its role is to facilitate the process of future ready. Schools that are built on the foundations of just and fair are schools that provide the opportunity to be fully valued regardless of the color of skin, ethnicity, or culture. This is about individuals. This is about human lives.

What exists now are programs and systems built on a person's disadvantage. Not to continue to beat the same drum, but to maintain these systems, we must continue to have people with disadvantages. Persons must be willing to stay disconnected from their essence. Of course, we know people are not "*opting in*" to stay disconnected from their truest self, but this is the result of conditioned behavior over time like the people in the small town. This is where bias and misleading belief originates. Not only beliefs we form about ourselves, but beliefs we form about others, and conversely, the belief of others formed about you.

We recall the cycle of broken people and broken systems. When fractured ways of doing and being are perpetuated, it results in broken systems feeding into another broken system. The persistence of brokenness creates over-pronounced and unmanageable fragmentation and chaos. This is what must change for a true reset and healing to happen. This is what must be dismantled.

Chasing and funding "*trauma gone wild*" symptoms is not only unsustainable but leaves you questioning motives. Solutions must be systemic, sustainable, scalable, and with regard for all those involved. We must be able to develop systems, processes, and supports that empower and equip, not further complicate, or capitalize on.

We need sound solutions embedded with empowerment that transcend and segment the fragmentated systems. Only then will we be able to produce solvency and wellbeing for all. When we can reset equitable foundations in education then we will put a stop to the spread of inequities. When we can do this, we will unlock the economy, and not just for some.

This begins to happen when we address the unresolved trauma in our own personal lives. Until then, we will continue to look through a skewed lens to determine what is just and fair. If we continually stayed stirred up and angry about everything, we will not be able to see just and fair. Not only will there be no semblance of just and fair, but we will continue to put ourselves in a position of vulnerability (*and not the good kind Brene' Brown talks about*). Bryan Stevenson, founder of Equal Justice Initiative (EJI), says that justice can never come from a place of fear and anger. He shares "*I am persuaded fear and anger are the essential ingredients of injustice, inequality, and oppression.*" As easy as it and instinctive as it can be to respond with anger, it's not the answer and to Stevenson's point only serves to fuel what we don't want.

**THE RESET**

**U**

This is not reform.
This is reestablishing foundations
and it begins with you.

We must begin as systems of government, communities of practice, and sectors of society to work together to mend this breach and not continue to prop it up. It begins with you and me. It is time for the education reset. It is time to learn from the past. It is time to do what we should have done from the beginning—establish equitable foundations, so that we can ensure flourishing futures.

# Chapter Two: The Problem—Macro

*From Personal Pain to Institutional Injustice*

## *Integrating the Shift*

1. In what ways have you seen unresolved trauma and systemic fragmentation feed into another system?
2. What is the cost of confusing developmental delay with disability, particularly for children in trauma?
3. Reflect on a time when you have felt like your "true ability" was misjudged because of internal or external conditions you were experiencing?
4. What might be some of the dangers of using standardized assessments to make life-altering decisions for students in stressful states?
5. What might it look like to stop "*chasing trauma symptoms*" and instead design for human flourishing?

# PART II
# A SOLUTION

# CHAPTER THREE
# THE PURPOSE

In this chapter, I lay out the deeper **purpose** behind resetting education: it's not just about reform—it's about **healing** society. I call for dismantling systems that were built on trauma, fragmentation, and inequity, and replacing them with life-giving, trauma-resilient structures rooted in truth, justice, and coherence. I introduce essential elements of this reset—like closing the gap between perceived capacity and true ability, creating coherent systems, and improving outcomes for students, schools, and communities. I emphasize that personal healing is not optional; it's the engine for systemic change. Without truth, empathy, and integrity, there can be no real equity. The reset begins when we stop systematizing dysfunction—and start systematizing healing.

# CHAPTER THREE
# THE PURPOSE

**About that promise to help heal.** With the same intentionality we have structuralized and institutionalized brokenness and chosen to benefit from it, we must by that same intentionality, disburden people, a system, and society by systematizing healing, and systems, processes, and programs that are just and lead to and foster flourishing.

Let's start here. The hard-to-face reality is that school climate is a function of school culture. School culture is the shared values, beliefs, and practices within a school community and is an outcome of a school's shared vision. When the shared vision produces a positive school culture, the school climate becomes one of healing, inclusivity, and equity, all driven by the set of shared core values and a commitment by all to live them out in authentic and integrous ways. Living them out, not because there is special program that tells you to receive a funding stream you must do x, y, and z, but you do it because it's the right thing to do. It is what humans do for other humans. It is what trauma-resilient systems and processes support and facilitate. It is what is required if we are going to interrupt the historical and generational trauma and the systemic inequities mass-produced because of it.

Schools committed to the reset commit to:

- Closing the gap between perceived capacity and true ability,
- Creating paths of coherence,
- Shifting outcomes,
- Doing what is just and fair, and
- Healing and restoration.

Healing requires intentional tools, not empty words or even good intentions.

**Closing the gap between perceived capacity and true ability.**

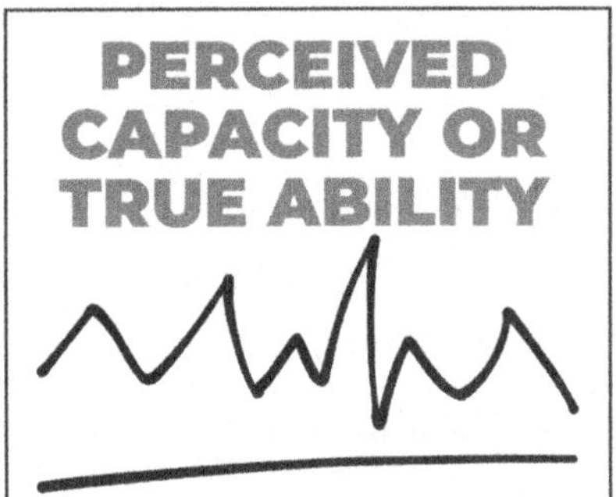

What you see in a moment is a culminating view of what you haven't seen over time OR what remains to be seen. Look beyond.

As you will recall from our brief discussion on the Blueprint for Trauma's Comprehensive Expression, trauma interferes with and disrupts the signals in our brain.

Let's go back to signals crossed. Imagine your brain as an air traffic control system, and each neuron or brain region as an aircraft. The brain sends signals to direct actions, like processing information, or regulating internal functions, much like how air traffic controllers direct the movement of planes in the airspace. If the signals are clear, the "planes" can reach their destinations safely and efficiently. If the signals are not clear, two planes might mistakenly be directed toward the same runway, because the controller issued unclear instructions.

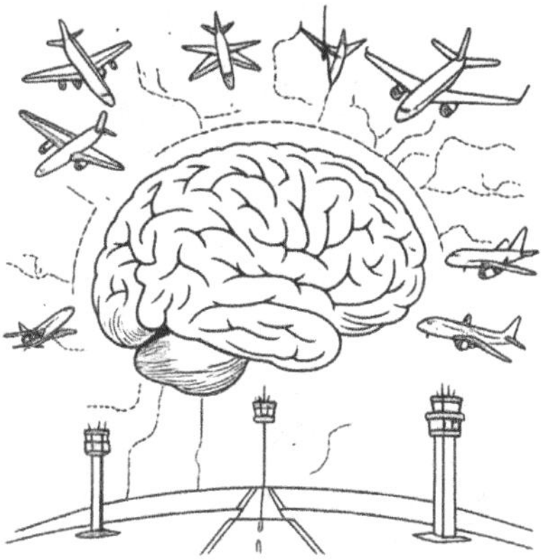

If the system works properly, there's harmony—smooth air traffic flow. But if signals are mixed up, it can lead to chaos, mistakes, or dangerous outcomes, whether in the brain or in air traffic. The goal is not to accommodate scrambled signals, although you may have to adapt in the short term to an interim pattern. The goal is to bring the signals back online operating at their optimum. This is what is going on in the classroom and this is where the work of reflex integration, rhythm and auditory processing and more comes in.

When we close the gap between perceived capacities and true abilities, we shut the trap door of misinterpretation, misrepresentation, and misdiagnosis that results in the ability to report such egregious statistics like 85% of incarcerated youth having learning disabilities (NCD, 2015). Closing this gap, at the school level, requires creating paths of coherence in service and instructional delivery.

**Creating paths of coherence.** If we are going to interrupt the errant and inequitable pattern, then we must first significantly reduce the multiplied effect of the fragmentation in school operations that continue to feed it.

**PATHS OF COHERENCE**

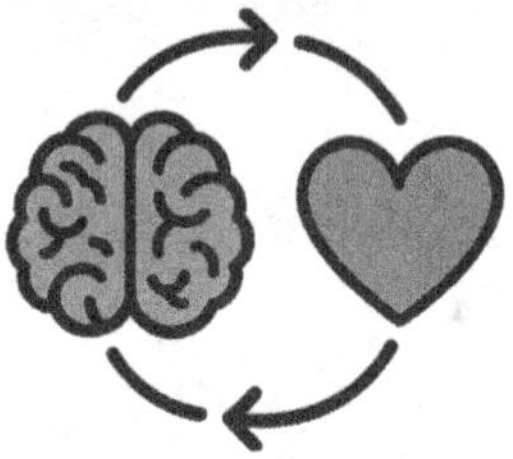

When alignment and order lock into place, they give you the courage to build toward a flourishing future.

This starts by examining each of the components of the operation, the functionality of each, and more importantly the interplay of the different components and different functions to each other. When programs, initiatives, positions, funding streams, and more have related outcomes and functions but are extremely siloed and disconnected this leads to the continued cycle of fragmentation and incongruence.

There must be measures at all levels of the operation to disburden the system from the immersive influence trauma has had on education's delivery of services and the educators, students, families, and communities, it impacts and represents. We need programs, interventions, and approaches that address the power levers of engaged parents and caregivers, regulated brains, and assets-based students.

Creating paths of coherence in schools, agencies, and organizations by addressing the fragmentation and incongruence among and within the delivery of services is the "*putting things in right order part*". This requires implementing key strategies that ensure continuity among functions and processes and then doing the integrous work of maintenance. The equitable and just delivery of services can only come from equitable systems and foundations.

**Shifting outcomes.** The reset will require making priority the equipping of educators, resource officers, school counselors, school psychologists and others to understand the integrative reality of unresolved trauma on and in their work; understanding how symptoms of trauma mimic what is thought to be signs of learning disabilities, special needs, and defiant behaviors (D'Andrea, et. al, 2012).

When you do this integrative work within the context of education, you will shift outcomes:

- student outcomes,
- school outcomes,
- community outcomes, and
- economic outcomes.

**Student outcomes.** When you can provide a customizable solution designed to support the way a child learns giving them true access to learning and discovery, incongruence and fragmentation begin to diminish.

**School outcomes.** When you address the fragmentation and incongruence in program delivery the quality and effectiveness of the programs increase. Funding and investments become money well spent and impact becomes sustainable.

**Community outcomes.** Schools that are committed to embedding the strategies of engaged parents, regulated brains, and assets-based students, experience long-term and sustainable impact and become a value-added member of their community.

**Economic outcomes.** When you impact student potential and grow their emotional and intellectual capacity in a purpose-driven direction, you increase their ability to participate as a positive, contributing, and constructive citizens in society.

**Doing what is just and fair.** As pointed out, in a society of an ecosystem of systems, education is the forerunner. If we are solving for systemic inequities, this requires building just and fair into the foundation. Families from different ethnicities, cultures, and socioeconomic status send their children to school every day with the expectation of receiving an equitable education.

**Healing and restoration.** In Montgomery, Alabama, stands The Legacy Museum carrying a tagline of *From Slavery to Mass Incarceration*. This museum represents the work and life's calling of The Esteemed Esquire, Mr. Bryan Stevenson and the Equal Justice Initiative (EJI). Walking through this incredible work of historical art and presentation, captioned with some of the most unconscionable recollections of depravity - the purest of evil – you are left asking *what must precede a person's ability to rationalize, willfully and knowingly, committing such unfathomable acts, deliberately putting another person or entire people group in harm's way for their own gain*?

> **NOTE**: Not to be forgotten, and as equally as important, are the stories from the Holocaust Museum or the First Americans Museum (FAM), all sharing the history of lives lost and origin stories stolen. All lives are equally valuable. Red, and yellow, black, brown, and white.

The pathway to healing and equity begins with removing the narratives that work to keep people in inequitable states. But first comes honesty, empathy, and understanding. We must first acknowledge and address the root of racial categorization that has led to the dehumanizing of people of color. We must (1) break the generational cycles, (2) heal the cognitive impact of trauma early, and (3) reverse the deficit messaging that has been created by taking historical and generational trauma and embedding it into structures and systems.

In 2024, I was asked to share at a conference happening in Toronto. The conference was focused on EDI in the Workplace. I was asked to present on Rebranding Education. "*Yes, please.*" Understanding the context of the conference, I framed my presentation accordingly sharing several of the sentiments I am sharing here. The events in history that took place for the social construct of racism to be institutionalized and systematized took much thought and many years. It also took much complacency and complicity.

When I had finished presenting, the host gave opportunity for some of the attendees to share feedback, thoughts, or ask questions. One of participants simply said, "*thank you for saying what we are all afraid to say.*" (It made me think of my friends who show up to work contradicting their own selves.) Then an older indigenous gentleman left me speechless, when he asked, "*Where were you 400 to 500 years ago*?" It was a sobering, and humbling kind of moment. Another reminder to keep going. We create our programs, file our suits, walk the streets, hoping someone will hear us, see us—because that is what we really want. However, in my humble opinion—and its only my opinion, the best of programs, the most valid of suits, and the most purposeful walks, will not bring the systemic solution that is needed. The programs will help some, the suits will be a just reward – even if momentarily – and the walks will help us feel like we did something, but it won't be a lasting change and that's what we need. We have these errant expectations that others know and feel about a thing the same way that we do or funnier still that they should. It ensures a steady flow of people jumping into foxholes or ditches or worse.

We must remember what we learned about trauma, it is not the event that is the worst thing, rather the lie that we believe because of it. Believing the lies, we continue—individually and as a collective—to empower the weakening of mind, soul, and body, literally.

Attempting to relegate the address of the systemic impact of trauma outside of education is only evidence of the fragmentation and incongruence it has created.

It is time for a reset in the education system where the schools are positioned ready to educate, the educators are empowered and equipped ready to teach, and the students are considered as individuals ready to learn and as an outcome, ready to contribute. This is our purpose, now on to the plan.

# Chapter Three: The Purpose

## *Systematizing Healing through Coherence and Integrity*

### *Integrating the Reset*

1. What are some strategies that could help "systematize healing" in education?

2. What's the difference between a "perceived capacity" and "true ability" in a student?

3. What are the risks of continuing to operate with fragmentation and incongruence?

4. What aspect of "coherence" do you feel most called to influence or build?

5. What would a healing-centered school or team culture look like to you?

# CHAPTER FOUR
# THE PLAN

In Chapter Four, I share **the plan** to reset education's foundation through a trauma-resilient, coherence-based approach. I introduce the **Universal Equity Pedagogy (UEP)**—a framework that reconnects identity, learning, and systems. I emphasize that true transformation requires both inner healing and external system redesign. By addressing generational trauma and honoring personal stories, students begin to see themselves through a lens of strength rather than deficit. I also introduce a system-wide tool to move us from fragmented interventions to integrated, purpose-driven solutions. This chapter calls on educators and leaders to anchor all change in justice, coherence, and truth—so we can finally create learning environments that unlock human potential.

# CHAPTER FOUR
# THE PLAN

If the effects of poverty and trauma can have such devastating and long-lasting effects, then the beginnings of children must be a top priority.

If we are going to remain a society that functions by way of an ecosystem of systems, then ensuring sound and equitable foundations in the systemic beginnings of education must be non-negotiable.

If we are going to tout that education is the answer to poverty, then we must make the changes necessary to interrupt and mitigate the effects of poverty and trauma on learning, and its subsequent impact on the public health and prosperity of a nation.

To facilitate this kind of reset in the predecessor system of education will require a multi-layered approach:

- Authorization and Support of Legislation and Policy,
- Address of Problem-Blindness, and
- Implementation and Sustainability of a Systemic Solution

## Legislation and Policy

It's time to choose healing: personally, organizationally, and systemically. It's time for a different kind of governance. It's time to abandon the strategy of altering formulas and numbers to guarantee the supply chain (funding stream) of a broken system. Instead of formulas that incentivize failure, it's time to create a new formula that promotes prosperity for all. It's time to stop shuffling students through an education system that leaves them as victims of life's circumstances. **It's time to start valuing and seeing students as a human life worthy of flourishing, championed by a new paradigm that says, "you can, you will, and we are here to make sure that you do."** It's time to return to the way it should have always been – education built on equitable foundations.

This is achievable - but only with the commitment of authentic, honest, and courageous leaders and decision-makers involved in government and education who will enact legislation and policy aligned with the current realities. Success depends on funding and supporting programs that reinforce, rather than undermine, the goals of a systemic solution that addresses the deep impact poverty and trauma have on students, families, and the education system itself. In addition, higher education institutions must adapt to prepare current and future educators to thrive—and find purpose—within the evolving landscape of education.

It will take legislation and policy that not only support needed change but actively incentivizes it—driven by leaders committed to building just systems that disrupt, rather than perpetuate, inequities. For example, the school-to-prison pipeline highlighted earlier represents a cycle of policies and practices that continue to lead to negative outcomes for students, including arrests, suspensions, expulsions, and involvement with the juvenile or criminal justice systems.

Addressing these historical and systemic issues and disparities require advocating policy changes, implementing strategies that are trauma-resilient, thus culturally responsive, and providing support services that address early the issue of brain readiness.

Reallocating funding and authority to the individual states provides the perfect opportunity to redefine education formulas that reflect whole family programming and preventative measures early. State education agencies have a strategic opportunity to rebuild the foundations of education with a student-centered and equity-driven vision.

To reduce the risks of misinterpretation, misrepresentation, and misdiagnosis, state boards of education must initiate a comprehensive review of all educational job descriptions and assignments. Given what history has taught us—and what trauma research now confirms—this is no longer optional. Every role in education must be re-evaluated through the lens of trauma's impact, with a clear focus on how it can contribute to healing rather than harm.

We must ensure that responsibilities across the system—whether in the classroom, administration, or student support—are aligned with trauma-resilient practices. This includes embedding clear expectations and competencies into roles such as, but not limited to, Classroom Educators, School Resource Officers, Special

Education Coordinators, School Social Workers, and Education Associates for School Climate.

When such roles fail to even mention, let alone require, trauma-resilient approaches, we are neglecting a critical layer of protection and failing the very students we aim to serve. Real change demands the intentional implementation of policies that prioritize early intervention and courageous and reciprocal leadership at every level. **Ensuring paths of coherence from the foundation of the system, turns funding from waste into investment. We need legislation and policy change that support this.**

In 2016, the same year my doctorate was conferred, the federal government began efforts to make sure we were languaging around "*trauma-informed*", but we were at a loss of how to live it out. If you have ever read anything I have written you probably heard this story. At the end of 2016, I was invited to a Congressional Briefing[12] where legislators were advocating for the trauma language in legislation and policy. One of the panelists at this briefing was the esteemed Dr. Colleen Cichetti. She was the psychologist at the Chicago's Children's Hospital. In addition to the statistics, she shared that day, she told us that in the span of one year the waiting list for children to be seen for mental health issues at the hospital had doubled from 400 to 800. Then she said, "*We do not have enough mental health workers to work our way out of this problem.*" I immediately thought to myself, *because this is not the problem*. Remember, "*chasing trauma gone wild*"

12 [U.S. Senator Heidi Heitkamp]. (2016, December 1). Public Policies to Improve Coordination, Prevention, and Response to Childhood Trauma [Video]. https://www.youtube.com/watch?v=I21l-8GH4S58&t=774s

symptoms. This was not meant in any way a rejection or rebuttal to Dr. Cichetti's statement, but further validation of my hypothesis.

Around this same time, the conversation around social and emotional learning was making its way to the forefront, although it had been around for years. My concern was that we would lose sight of what needed to happen to address trauma and one more time put a demand on educators that they were not able to bear.

I began a search of legislation having to do with social and emotional learning to ensure the language and crosswalk around the origin of trauma and its direct correlation to SEL outcomes were clear. In my search, I found a piece of legislation called the SELF (Social and Emotional Learning for Families) Act that had been sponsored by Congressman Tim Ryan. I reached out to his office to inquire of the status and to share that, although excited about the possibility of the legislation, I had a concern that there was no mention of trauma. The absence of the language in the legislation underscored my suspicion about the disconnect and lack of understanding. I shared my concerns with the legislative aide, asking the question, "*how can we talk about social and emotional learning standards and not address its antithesis of trauma*?". My position was and is that we can't hold teachers and students accountable for Social and Emotional Learning (SEL) standards or even have expectations of competencies being attained when we have not adequately addressed and equipped for the origins that dictate the undesired outcomes. You should be remembering Maya Angelou's quote.

In 2019, I decided to draft the legislation that I believed would systemically address trauma in education. There had been some effort, as mentioned, to include "*trauma-informed*" language, but it didn't feel, to me, that it went far enough. It didn't address the root cause in my estimation. "*Trauma-informed*" infers an add-on, but what was needed was "*trauma-resilient*", something that was integrated throughout all the parts. Quick sidebar, an add-on versus an integration speaks to the reality of fragmented and siloed operations. It is like comparing lip service to heart change or mind shift. Little did I know as I prepared the legislation, that we would soon be in the middle of a global crisis, and instead of addressing trauma, we would create more of it. We were constantly being pelted with the messages from the CDC's rendition of John Travolta's number one hit, *Staying Alive, Staying Alive.* While legislator's focused on other pressing matters, I placed the idea of the legislation on hold, waiting for, let's say, a *kinder, more gentle* time.

In 2022, a state legislator offered to bring the legislation to the Education Committee of which she chaired. Promptly, we received pushback from legislative counsel stating that what the legislation was proposing would impact federal funding. *Well, well, well, would you look at that?* Here we are, federal funding impacted. In hindsight, it might have been the wiser choice to, albeit federal funding impacted, instead of worrying about saving our asses, I mean line items, to have been more concerned about saving the children.

When the mission of the U.S. Department of Education or any entity, for that matter, is not met, we say they are mission adrift. When the U.S. Department of Education is mission adrift, it greatly impacts the individuals within the system to produce and contribute to and participate in the economy of the world they live in.

Don't get me wrong, we need systems, processes from which to operate, but they are in service to people. If education becomes an industry – which it has - then what does that make our children?

Flourishing societies promote an education system that integrates into its design the support and space for empowerment that help students access the discovery and the development of their strengths, passions, and interests necessary for making their contribution in the world. Recent reports on where the U.S. education system ranks, clearly lets us know, we have not been doing our job, as a system.

While we may be currently dismantling what we know as the U.S. Department of Education and returning oversight to the States, we can't walk away from 40 years of carnage without hopefully making some type of retribution in the way of supporting the systemic solution. If you came in my house and broke something, it only makes sense that you would take responsibility and fix what you broke. That's all.

Remember, the discussion on normalized dysfunction in our personal lives. The mass fragmentation created in education from the multiplied effect of unresolved trauma from all the stakeholders would be an example of the micro to macro effect and how normalized dysfunction is being played out on a very large institutional scale. Forty years of messaging from a broken system that is mission adrift impacts the minds and thought processes over time. This mass effect of normalized dysfunction creating what is called problem blindness. Simultaneously, as we put in place legislation and policy, we will also then have to address the issue of problem blindness.

## Problem-Blindness

It is difficult to fix what you have been conditioned not to see.

With needed change to legislation and policy in process, we begin to address the heart issue that brought us here. Addressing this heart issue will require the removal of our proverbial blindfold. The proverbial blindfold like the large disgusting bandaid that has been left far too long on an ugly and festering sore. This blindfold or unwillingness to see and recognize, let alone address, has led to an erosion of societal foundations. The idea that some humans are of lesser value than others, has allowed for the introduction of many horrendous acts and ideologies. Over time, this breach in our collective psyche became the soil from which governmental and societal systems emerged.

In Upstream: The Quest to Solve Problems Before They Happen, Dan Heath addresses problem blindness by exploring how individuals and organizations can shift their focus from reactive problem-solving to proactive prevention. Problem blindness occurs when individuals or systems fail to recognize a problem as a problem, often because they've grown so accustomed to its presence that it feels normal or inevitable. This blindness keeps people reacting to the symptoms instead of questioning the system that produces them. In the book, Heath presents strategies for addressing systemic issues by tackling root causes instead of merely managing symptoms. These principles can significantly benefit the education system by fostering a culture of prevention and long-term thinking.

Maybe you are thinking, can you be more specific? How about this? Problem blindness in education arises when systemic challenges—such as inequities in resources, teacher burnout, and chronic absenteeism—are seen as unavoidable realities rather than solvable issues. This mindset normalizes disparities (normalized dysfunction) and is what prevents meaningful systemic change.

To counteract problem blindness, schools must avoid tunnel vision, which leads to reactive crisis management. Instead, educators and leaders can adopt proactive strategies such as early assessments, personalized interventions, and long-term planning that prioritizes student well-being and teacher sustainability.

Addressing upstream issues also requires proactive collaboration among schools, families, and community organizations to tackle root causes like poverty and food insecurity. Building interdisciplinary teams within schools helps identify and support at-risk students before problems escalate.

Another critical step is to measure success differently, using prevention-focused indicators such as student engagement, early literacy, and attendance trends—rather than relying solely on standardized test scores. I think we all know this in theory. The challenge and the charge is to put the measures in place to ensure that we are doing what we know.

Ultimately, overcoming problem blindness demands systemic thinking: reevaluating policies and structures, reducing teacher turnover through support programs, and promoting equity by reallocating resources and creating inclusive curricula. By shifting from reactive to preventative approaches, and by recognizing that educational systems can be redesigned, we can address root causes and build a more equitable, sustainable future for all learners.

Implementing legislation and policy as discussed above will put a demand on addressing the challenges problem blindness creates. Next, and while those things are happening, we will need integrous leaders to show up and implement the systemic solutions with their strategies and processes to bring and sustain the much-needed change.

## Systemic Solution

Education that realizes story. A way of learning that works for everyone.

When I realized that students were being misdiagnosed with learning disabilities, I took this as a direct affront to their personhood. Understanding then, what has only become more magnified now, about the brokenness of our education system, this, for me, became a matter of justice. My pursuit of justice through innovation of a solution in the predecessor system of education gave birth to the Universal Equity Pedagogy (UEP)[13].

13 Universal Equity Pedagogy: the systemic solution for social change and eco-

UEP is the social pedagogy to address an education system that, given its best efforts, continues to exacerbate and perpetuate inequitable and inexcusable outcomes. Inequitable and inexcusable outcomes filtered from the predecessor system of education into every other system in society, continuing its path of fragmentation and incongruence.

A social pedagogy is one that aims to encourage a strong sense of community and educates both children and adults to facilitate positive relations among education, individuals, and society.[14] UEP does this.

UEP and the methodologies, systems, and frameworks that support it represent a theory of change able to guide the shifts in education that are so desperately needed. Systems and schools that embrace the shift possess certain foundational understandings:

**Foundational Understandings**

- Children and students are the centerpiece of learning and the work of transformative education.
- Learning is a relationally mediated activity.
- Trauma is a universal phenomenon.
- Trauma's impact has been systemically immersed in society.
- Persons with unaddressed and unresolved trauma cannot, or find it difficult to, act or behave in equitable ways.
- Unaddressed trauma and its impact and influence are impediments to learning and development.

nomic prosperity (white paper)

14 Eichsteller, G., & Holthoff, S. (2011). Social Pedagogy as an ethical orientation towards working with people—Historical perspectives. *Children Australia*, *36*(4), 176-186.

- Labeling, of any kind, is premature when the work of eliminating barriers to a student's true giftings and abilities has not been addressed and fully exhausted,
- Trauma is not a respecter of culture, race, or socioeconomic status.
- Poverty can serve as an exacerbator of trauma's impact. Affluency can serve as a mitigator and mediator working together to hide the appearance of trauma's impact.
- Emotional, behavioral, social, and mental influences from unaddressed trauma are disproportionately represented in black and brown children.
- Emotional, behavioral, social, and mental influences from unaddressed trauma are compounded in communities that are impoverished, regardless of race.

The foundation's sustainability depends on commitments and drivers that protect its integrity.

**Commitments and Drivers**

For UEP to be successful, it must reside in an environment supportive of its tenets and committed to the implementation of key strategies in their education environments and learning spaces:

- Identifying areas within their comprehensive delivery of services that are fragmented and incongruent,
- Addressing internally and externally—among all stakeholders—mindsets that would perpetuate fragmentation and incongruence,
- Training all staff in critical areas that support successful implementation and sustainability of equitable, congruent

delivery of educational services,
- Implementing a process for intentional and effectual engagement of parents/families,
- Broadening the definition and role of teacher/educator to be more of a facilitator-coach,
- Restoring teacher/educator autonomy to the classroom and ensuring load-distribution is equal among all stakeholders,
- Supporting educators in their pursuit of meaning-making in their craft and calling—teachers should feel fulfilled and energized by their work, not depleted,
- Teaching and interacting with students respective of the individual child and their context, with the ability and willingness to address the barriers that serve as impediments to learning, and therefore, access to education.

The commitments above serve as UEP indicators, with system drivers defined as follows:

- Driver #1. Ensure the contiguous incorporation of variables across all functions that impact the whole.
- Driver #2. Address the health and wellbeing of the child.
- Driver #3. Draw on, partner with, and support those persons closest to the child.
- Driver #4. Ensure the order and functionality of the preceding tasks have been completed.
- Driver #5. Ensure that all stakeholders have been invited to the table and all perspectives considered, all while keeping the students themselves central to the entire process.

**Key Components**

The UEP components of CIRCLES, TIERS, and SPHERES receive their direction from within the student's learning story. Learning stories (Carr & Lee 2012) are exactly what they sound like—using storytelling to describe or guide the learning process, and within UEP stories intentionally informed by key knowings and understandings to the individual child's success. We call it Learning STRY. Simply put, the student's story and context are the path hidden in plain sight. You can think of it as a personalized hero's journey. This human centered, design-for-life approach in an education environment—whether home, school, or classroom — is eco-shifting. Learning STRY supports co-creation and co-design with all stakeholders to reach the goals necessary for flourishing and building strong communities as prescribed in a social pedagogy like UEP.

The Learning STRY and healing model provided within UEP helps shift to inquiry-based, trauma-resilient instruction away from a delivery of content that is outside the context of someone's lived experience. The intentionality around the individual is what makes it inclusive. UEP is aimed at transformation, not performance only. This mindset will help replace test-only systems with systems that can assess using narrative portfolios and wellness indicators.

Instead of making equity and inclusion something that creates division, embrace it as something that brings healing and transformation.

CIRCLES serve as gears ensuring the forward movement amongst all the parts (people, practices, processes, products, and principles). Next, TIERS represents preparedness and scaffolding toward readiness outlined within the Grounded Learning Framework (GLF). Finally, this preparedness leads to the positive

| TIER | PRIORITY FOCUS | PRIORITY DRIVER | PRIORITY INTEGRATION |
|---|---|---|---|
| LEVEL 1 ZERO – 3 **FIND** | Early Brain and Child Development | Attachment | Regulation |
| LEVEL 2 PreK – Gr. 3 **BUILD** | Core of Four / Foundational Literacy | Attachment | Regulation |
| LEVEL 3 Gr. 4 – 6 **DISCOVER** | Core of Me / Literacy of Self | Application | Connection |
| LEVEL 4 Gr. 7 – 12 **CONTRIBUTE** | Core of You / Literacy of Community | Agency | Multiplication |

*Figure 4. UEP Tiers © 2020-2025*

and constructive contribution students make in the different SPHERES of influence.

**Circles**

As we now understand, unaddressed childhood trauma in a student multiplied across millions impacts a system. This mass fragmentation has left education responding and building in very siloed ways. As stated, to offer a pedagogy that is equitable and applicable across all demographics and geographics, the reality of trauma's impact on learning and developed must be an integrative part of the solution. The answer is found through the process of reciprocity and reciprocal engagement led by reciprocal leaders. Leaders, staff, and educators as groupings of circles gathered around to support and facilitate the success of individual students and their families as well as the success of one other. Reciprocity is all about turning silos into circles. The use of circles is a way of ensuring the inclusion and integration as well as closing the gap around all the processes and systems that might affect a student.

As inferred, the circles design applies to people, practices, processes, products, and principles. It is also applied in the design of learning and workspaces. We already see this applied in differential groupings, professional learning communities, and more.

**Tiers**

Within the TIER component, there are four tiers which are core. They are labeled as FIND, BUILD, DISCOVER, and CONTRIBUTE. The framework allows for identification of specific and intentional areas of emphasis within each developmental stage. Each tier is scaffolded one on another. Regardless of the stage of implementation, measures are taken to identify and close the developmental gaps (expand capacity). The longer the delay in addressing the gap, the higher the risk of its widening, and the increase likelihood of costly and inequitable outcomes.

**Tier 1: Early Development.** Ensuring a sound foundation is the "*don't pass go*" of the first tier, FIND, which focuses on identifying and building sound and equitable foundations. Tier 1 is about *finding* our bearings. A grounded life supports grounded learning, which requires identifying a student's interrupters and missing pieces. Research shows that trauma symptoms often resemble learning disabilities, masking children's true abilities. As Dr. Bruce Perry notes, learning is state-dependent. When we connect these insights, it becomes clear why children from trauma-impacted environments may struggle to perform at their full potential. The area of focus for the FIND tier is Early Brain and Child Development, where we note the priority of emotional and cognitive regulation. Assessment of this factor is critical to equitable foundations because if a child has a capacity issue, it could very well be an issue of development, not ability. **Lack of evidence of a skill doesn't mean that skill cannot be developed, it only means it has not been given the opportunity to develop—an extremely important point to make note of since education is, after all, all about opportunity.** The gap between developmental capacity and learning ability lies in the limitations and impediments created by the impact of stress and trauma on the brain. The impact of stress and trauma mask, and thus make it easy to misinterpret, a student's true learning abilities.

In both the FIND and BUILD tiers, strong focus is given to embedding the construct of REGULATION. As shared, a dysregulated brain has difficulty learning and processing. If a regulated brain is the optimal ideal for learning and growing, then why would we build on anything less? Embedding regulatory activities—ensuring a sound foundation—will help address this potential interruption. The priorities of Early Brain and Child Development as well as Regulation is always supported by, and naturally connected to, the domain of ATTACHMENT, which is highlighted in the first two tiers. Everything we do should support the foundational understandings of UEP. Attachment translates into engagement and involvement with the home (parents, caregivers, and families). When we are talking about interrupting and mitigating for the impact of trauma, parents (caregivers and families) are an indisputable part of the equation. This makes it incumbent upon the school system to include the family and caregivers in the educational process. Ensuring a secure environment is being provided, and that those responsible for providing it are getting the supports they need, is required for the foundational work taking place in the FIND and BUILD tiers.

Schools receive multiple streams of funding every year that require the involvement and engagement of parents and families. Unfortunately, too many schools do little more than minimal, surface activities to meet this deliverable. **The lack of meaningful engagement with a student's primary social support system must change.** Failure to do so is a choice to ignore the research and science, and this avoidance will only lead to continued fragmentation and incongruence, not to mention misappropriation of the funds received to do otherwise.

When schools understand that unaddressed trauma is representative of the broken foundation and that it is generational in nature, then healthy attachments and relationships are the initial steps for managing the breach. This is a human-centered, student-centric response.

**Tier 2: Foundational Literacy.** The BUILD tier is about scaffolding on top of the sound foundation that has begun, continuing to emphasize and strengthen everything addressed in the FIND tier. The focus of the BUILD tier is what we refer to as the Core of Four. These are like the four wheels on our magic school bus.

1. Literacy,
2. Numeracy,
3. Creative Thinking, and
4. Critical Thinking.

**Literacy and Numeracy.** All education research and literature identify the need for a strong foundation of literacy skills in both words and numbers. Research supporting the critical need to master these skills early spans decades. The perpetual benchmark of "*able to read by the end of 3rd Grade*", that for some reason we continue to stumble over rather than reach, despite the voluminous research and a host of programs established to address it and the small fortune invested, should give pause for much thought. One thought might be, "*perhaps these children have dysregulated brains resulting from unaddressed trauma that is impeding their learning.*" To restate what we already know, Literacy empowers. It equips students with the ability to understand content and to grasp concepts, enabling them to discover new ideas and deepen learning. Literacy levels correlate directly with issues such as poverty, workforce development, and health, to name a few.

In UEP, schools pause to ensure the student is centered within their Learning STRY. Instead of feeling unprepared and isolated, we identify the paths of coherence informed by our knowings and understandings. Reading, for example, becomes tied to the student's own interests and voice. The student sees themselves as a storyteller and a learner, not a struggling reader. **This is agency**. The school adjusts to the student's needs rather than forcing the student to adjust to the needs of the broken and misaligned structure and system. **This is equity**.

Numeracy is defined as the ability to work with numbers in everyday situations. Its application covers all areas of life. The inability to understand numbers and how they are used renders a person vulnerable. Numeracy is foundational to success in math applications and advanced math such as algebra. Research tells us that students who do not complete advanced math classes are more likely to drop out of high school. Again, organizations, resources, and research abound highlighting the important correlation between numeracy and life and workforce skills.
**Creative and Critical Thinking.** Partnering with and building upon Literacy and Numeracy is Creative and Critical Thinking. Curricula designed to emphasize Creative and Critical Thinking addresses hemispheric integration, which is key to trauma healing. Childhood trauma's impact changes the architecture of a child's brain. The *corpus callosum*, which is the mediator between the functionality of the right and left hemispheres, becomes constricted, negatively influencing the communication between the two. Students with trauma encounter difficulty processing when learning tasks are

designed with disregard to the importance of strengthening hemispheric integration, especially when coupled with a traditional focus on left brain activity. The younger the child is, the less developed their expressive language will be. Even without specific knowledge of the trauma, tasks that target hemispheric integration build a child's cognitive capacity. Through approaches like reflex integration, somatosensory support, rhythm and auditory processing hemispheric integration begins to take place and creating coherence on a personal level begins to happen. Focus on Creative Thinking and right brain activities helps build the ability for expression, which unlocks the processes needed for a more balanced and functional brain. Greater success is achieved with the brain-friendly approach of right (creative) to left (critical), not left to right sequencing of tasks. In other words, a brain-friendly approach moves from context to details, not details to context. Details without context feeds fragmented and siloed thinking.

As mentioned, in the BUILD tier we continue to include, embed, and feature the constructs of REGULATION and ATTACHMENT to ensure and support the continuance of sound, early brain and child development while simultaneously mitigating for identified interrupters. **When you regulate the brain and put measures in place to support equitable foundations, you will stop the bleed of unconscionable proficiency rates. When you regulate the brain and put measures in place to support equitable foundations, you will not only "close the achievement gap", but you will also begin to close the gap between perceived capacity and true ability**. This is where you are implementing the work of Dr. Bruce Perry, Dr. Stuart Albon, Dr. Gabor Mate', Bonnie Brandes, and others, for example.

**Tier 3: Literacy of Self.** Scaffolding on top of the BUILD tier is DISCOVER. With the confidence of a healthy and regulated brain, coupled with strong foundational literacy and thinking skills, it is time to explore the Literacy of Self. After ensuring a firm foundation on which to extend the learning experience, it is time to create opportunities for extension and application. The understanding of strengths, passions, and interests facilitated in Tier 3 is key to continued development and the end goal of personal agency required for contribution. Students in Tier 3 are gaining the capacity to oversee their own journey. Self-determination theory posits that both extrinsic and intrinsic influences support—either positively or negatively—the three psychological needs of autonomy, competence, and relatedness. This is what the DISCOVER tier is all about. In the DISCOVER tier students are led to investigate their strengths and passions. Once identified, they begin to explore how these strengths, passions, and interests (autonomy) can intersect to build skills that will empower them to contribute positively and constructively to society in ways of their own choosing.

**"When students explore topics that are genuinely meaningful to them, inevitably amazing things happen."**

Trevor Mackenzie, Author, Inquiry Mindset

Students learn best in their own context (relatedness). Through this process of contextualizing learning, students begin to see the connections and applications to their own lives. If we want creative, self-motivated students, we must teach them in the way they learn about things that are important to them. The more applicable the instruction, the more effective and the deeper the learning experience, and the more successful the student (competence). Through *inquiry-based learning*, educators partner with students as facilitator-coaches to co-create and co-design personalized and contextualized learning experiences. Curriculum taught through personalized projects, guided by the student's Learning STRY, with an inquiry mindset, allows students to build on and refine their strengths, passions, and interests.

**Tier 4: Literacy of Community.** The CONTRIBUTE Tier is where students began to take ownership via their personal agency and own their unique contributions. We could say that they are now in the driver's seat of the magic school bus—that they have become self-determined. Their sense of belongingness and assurance in who they are allows them to locate themselves in the context of the larger story. They can now begin to turn their hearts and minds to how their gifts and talents can make an impact not only on their prosperity and wellbeing but to the benefit of the prosperity and wellbeing of the world around them.

Student projects and inquiry (cross-curricular) begin to center around solving problems and addressing needs in society. This is where assignment of practicums, service-learning, and intern opportunities are matched with mentors and partners. This is where we see the UEP component of SPHERES (see explanation below). The goal of Tier 4 is for students to *locate* themselves with a strong sense of personal agency, self-efficacy, and self-worth—and when ready—to go out and be a value-add to the world around them, depositing and multiplying the goodness of their "*best self.*"

**Spheres**

Students multiplying their best self into the lives and communities around them is where we see SPHERES at play. The component of SPHERES is found within and beyond the CONTRIBUTE tier. Students begin to engage in and identify *spheres of influence* and safe places in the community they would like to contribute. Depending on the desires and interests of the students, the level and sphere of where they want to contribute and become involved can vary. SPHERES could involve technology, healthcare, finances, city planning, agricultural, media, civic, community, and more. The geographic of contribution could be local, global, glocal, or somewhere in between. Wherever students find themselves, they see themselves as a positive, contributing, and constructive member of society making their unique imprint.

## Leader, Leader, Where for Art Thou Leader

As stated, but worth the underscore, a solution is only as good as the leadership that implements it. To be successful, reciprocal leaders must step forward. Reciprocal leaders are those, at every level, that are willing to boldly reject the normalization of generational, historical, and traumatic narratives that have left schools and communities desensitized, broken, and settling for the status quo.

Reciprocal leaders must confront the reality of the inequitable foundations in education and advocate for the change that is needed. At the school level, these reciprocal leaders are willing to embrace the challenge of doing what is within their power to provide an equitable foundation for students by beginning to:

- Create Paths of Coherence,
- Interrupt Misinterpretation, Misrepresentation, and Misdiagnosis, and
- Design and Build Forward for Sustained Congruence.

**Create Paths of Coherence**

The purpose of implementing a systemic solution like UEP within the trauma-immersed, predecessor system of education is to solve for coherence: personally, organizationally, and systemically. Patrick Lencioni, author and leader of The Table Group, shares that creating cohesion involves building trust, engaging conflict, taking action, establishing accountability, and pursuing common goals.[15] Designing and managing for coherence in a school or organization requires implementing key strategies authentically and intentionally as well as ensuring continuity across all the parts of the enterprise. Embracing the principle of integrative thinking and addressing inequities on the front end within a growth mindset is the necessary culturally responsive, inclusive approach, only then can our efforts have an effect.

Using a remediation (*making the remedy a priority*) tool built on the key drivers, schools can identify the connections and interplays in daily operations that directly impact the delivery of services.

Once you have the areas of incongruence identified, you can begin to map next steps forward. As we design our integration and

15 Lencioni, P. M. (2012). *The advantage: Why organizational health trumps everything else in business*. John Wiley & Sons.

execution plan, we are considering the strategies necessary to interrupt the cycle.

**Interrupts Misinterpretation, Misrepresentation, and Misdiagnosis**

In addition to the findings generated from the remediation tool, leaders must gather the information necessary for the disrupt and the shift to be successfully implemented. *First*, students who are trauma suspect must be identified. *Secondly and simultaneously*, the organization must be enabled to provide the approaches and interventions needed to address the impact of the trauma (brain development, regulation, attachment). As we do this, we will begin to establish the equitable foundations that shift the experience and outcomes of students, closing the gap between the challenge of perceived capacity and true ability.

**Identifies Students Who are Trauma Suspect**

Identifying students who display symptoms and behavior associated with trauma requires selecting a protocol for doing so, which includes choosing an instrument.

> **NOTE**: Rather than viewing "identifying" students—a term tied to past patterns of over- and misdiagnosis—we re-language to emphasize intentionality around recognizing areas for intervention that can shift students away from a deficit trajectory and toward capacity-building and growth.

One instrument, although most often used outside the education system—is the Child and Adolescent Needs and Strengths

(CANS)[16]. According to the lead developer, Dr. John Lyons, CANS is a multi-purpose tool that supports decision-making, which includes service planning to inform the delivery of services. This instrument can be used in elementary schools for the early identification of trauma with appropriate training and accommodations. The Functional Behavior Assessment (FBA) is another instrument used to identify challenging behaviors and their causes and as well as strategies to address them. The CANS and FBA can help guide conversations within the school team to inform the well-being of children and youth, identify their strengths and needs, and to inform strategies and best practices needed to position children back to a place where they are ready to learn.

Using the CANS, FBA or other instrument early as a tool to identify a student as *trauma suspect* brings the solution upstream, helping to avoid misinterpretation (leading to misrepresentation and misdiagnosis). A recommended protocol – if a child is *suspected* of having a learning disability (*because we now know that trauma symptoms mimic the same symptoms of many LD's*) with a priority placed on students living in poverty (*because we now know that poverty is a number one indicator of trauma*), they are provided an evaluation. If they "*test positive*" for the likelihood of trauma, they are given a classification of "Trauma-Suspect," and you take a predetermined amount of time to implement best practices to address and close the gap between developmental capacity and true ability. This is some of the information included in the draft legislation I have crafted. We wouldn't tell a child with a broken

16 https://www.cdss.ca.gov/inforesources/foster-care/cans/the-cans-tool/cans-resources

leg; *you will never be able to run a race*. No, we would mend the broken leg. I do understand science and research and the purpose of labels necessary to codify and categorize for understanding but am cautious when we take and make these labels identity markers. As an adult, with lingering effects of unresolved trauma, I was glad to have something to hang my *hypervigilant* and *easily startled* attributes on. It felt a little comforting at the time but what it served as was a locator so I could know where to start working and get to root of the problem.

In the process of executing your protocol and gathering your information, compassionate inquiry[17] and empathetic listening are applied, and stories are extracted to ensure that:

> (1) children are receiving the appropriate interventions and remedies for their specific needs.
> (2) developmental gaps are being mended.
> (3) mislabeling, misdiagnosis, and misappropriation are being avoided; and
> (4) systemic inequities are being interrupted.

Regardless of the instrument, the goal is to be preemptive and preventative. Why? Because equity – just and fair – means before not after.

**Provides Approaches and Interventions Needed to Address the Impact of the Trauma**

Addressing the impact of trauma requires a strength-based model. This in no way dismisses best practices in place but perhaps an

17 www.compassionateinquiry.com

opportunity to reevaluate the context in which they are presented and the sequence in which they are implemented. MTSS, the framework for providing academic, behavioral, and social-emotional support, would have measures, if not already in place, to ensure presentation and implementation are learner-centric and trauma-resilient.

For example, IEPs and 504 Plans often focus on deficits and compliance rather than student identity, story, or capacity. UEP is focused on student story integration. Instead of solely documenting impairments, teams incorporate a student's personal history, interests, and resilience markers into planning. Engaging in strengths mapping helps to reframe accommodations and goals around what the student can do and how they can thrive. A student with ADHD may be labeled as "*easily distracted*," but under UEP, their curiosity and divergent thinking become core assets. Their IEP includes projects that build on these strengths (e.g., inquiry-based learning or hands-on tasks). Often, IEP and 504 accommodations may not align with the student's developmental or trauma-related cognitive state. Through the lens of UEP, it would encourage assessments and supports aligned with neurosequential development ensuring strategies match brain readiness and regulation capacity. Schools can use regulation maps or trauma-informed learning readiness indicators to tailor services more effectively. Trauma-resilient spaces and other like strategies for those times when student are under pressure, for example, are worked into the 504 plans.

The bottom line is that we want to question and uncover what is beneath the behavior or academic struggles, investing on the front-end the time and intentionality to **understand the learner**

**and their needs**. I certainly realize that there are those that already engage in similar strategies and processes. I am not talking about something that is done in a small number of schools that are forward thinking but this is a universal embedded into the system. We know so much more now than we have in the past. It is the just thing to do.

For example, Brandes shares,

> *"Adding simple techniques and movements to connect, repair and activate these crucial connections can make the difference between learning and failure. Reflex integration creates the foundation for reading, writing, math, and other skills needed in the classroom. For example, when a reflex called Spinal Galant can is unintegrated conditions like ADHD can impede focus and organization. The Moro reflex can put one in fight or flight which can make eye tracking for reading difficult. The Asymmetrical Tonic Neck Reflex, ATNR, affects numerous skills like reading, handwriting, focus, and math."*

The point – there are solutions, strategies, and processes for addressing the needed reset. The challenge is to be intentional and integrous about implementing them and implementing them in the right order.

We need to be the educators and caring, emotionally stable adults we wanted when we were children. Before focusing on achievement, we need to ensure the systemic gaps of belonging and access have been addressed. We don't want to accommodate the gap but rather take inventory to help close the gap and fashion a unique path forward.

In my experience and observation, this involves the leveraging of three power levers:

1. Engaged Parents/Families (EP),
2. Regulated Brains (RB), and
3. Assets-Based Students (AS).

**1-Engaged Parents/Families (EP)**. The power lever of Engaged Parents/Families (EP) addresses the impediment of disengaged parents/families helping to dismantle the generational cycle. EP focuses on building and strengthening relationships with home. EP counters the disengagement so often seen in education.

When it comes to addressing inequities, nothing is more powerful than the ability to interrupt generational cycles through parent and family engagement. Dr. Gabor Mate' calls it downloading trauma from one generation to the next. The resulting miseducation from not systemically addressing the historical and systemic inequities and traumas has led to generational and structuralized cycles of institutionalism, marginalization, and disenfranchisement. To address this, we must reach back into the families—there is no other way. Although the opinions vary, the dismal outcomes cannot be argued. **Reaching back into the family with empowering, engaging, and equipping activities and strategies inside a multi-generational learning environment is a must-have.** Instead of attempting to keep parents and caregivers at arm's length, we should be hanging out signs that read **"If your child goes to school here, so do you!"**

Dr. Karen Mapp, for decades, has been sharing the research around the importance of the home environment and intentional parent and family engagement and its relationship to healthy, regulated brains and in turn, academic success. Therefore, we can say with confidence, that the science and research around the connection and relationship between Engaged Parents/Families (EP) and Regulated Brains (RB) is clear. Anything that jeopardizes the mother's emotional wellbeing (unaddressed trauma) may disrupt the child. This emotional stress on the mother interferes with infant brain development because it tends to interfere with attunement. Attunement—the sharing of emotional space—is necessary for the normal development of the brain pathways and neurochemical apparatus of attention and emotional self-regulation. Disruption to parent-child relationships can lead to the development of maladaptive behaviors and mental patterns[18]. Trauma most often than not is multigenerational. Remember, the "*before zero stuff*". As it cycles from one generation to the next, parent to child, stretching as Mate' so succinctly states "from the past into the future" and what we don't clean up now will be left to the next generation.

**2-Regulated Brains (RB).** Next, Regulated Brains (RB) addresses the cognitive impact of trauma interrupting emotional dysregulation and moving the student to a place ready to learn. RB is about relationship with self, restoring the connection lost at the impact of the trauma. RB counters the dysregulation. Addressing the dysregulation early directly impacts the emotions and behaviors, helping to position students in a place where they are cognitively ready to learn. The brain develops, processes, and

18 Maté, G. (2011). *Scattered minds: The origins and healing of attention deficit disorder*. Vintage Canada.

acts on incoming information in a sequential way—from bottom to top impacting other regions of the brain.[19] If students are in survival mode or operating out of the bottom part of their brain, it will be difficult for information to be received and processed. The impairment can negatively influence the cognitive processes required for learning in the classroom, including executive functioning, language, memory, attention, and integration.[20] In *What Happened to You?*[21], Perry stresses the importance of *the sequence of engagement*. He emphasizes that regulatory and somatosensory needs must be addressed before you can expect success with the cognitive. This is the looking to uncover what is beneath the behavioral and academic struggle piece. His strategies and approaches for addressing brain regulation and its impact on behavior and performance in a school setting can be found in the Neurosequential Modeling in Education (NME) he developed. One of my colleagues and school administrators in the State of Texas, Dr. Dinorah Bores, shared her experience with NME.

> "*Teaching students, parents, teachers, and staff how to regulate their brain has been a gamechanger. It has drastically reduced our discipline referrals. If we would have had these tools (regulating brains) sooner, we could also have prevented and reduced more special education referrals. This is the work of equity.*"

---

19 Perry, B.D. (2017, October 24-25). *NME Trauma Program Bootcamp*, Nashville, TN, United States.

20 Bonk, I. "Professional Development for Elementary Educators: Creating a Trauma-Informed Classroom." *Regent University*, ProQuest, 2016, pp. 1–169.

21 Perry, B.D., & Winfrey, O. (2021). *What happened to you? Conversations on trauma, resilience, and healing*. Flatiron Books.

As the Engaged Parents/Families (EP) power lever is related to Regulated Brains (RB), so the Regulated Brains (RB) power lever is related to the Assets-Based Students (AS) power lever. Research[22] shows a direct correlation between emotional regulation and agency. The confidence and social competence that comes from knowing your strengths, assets, and abilities and the pursuit of them in a personal context, creates agency.

**3-Assets-based Students (AS)**. The last power lever of Assets-Based Students (AS) disrupts the negative and deficit messaging replacing it with the strengths and assets that all children have to offer. Assets-Based Students (AS) is about relationship with others. Schools and educators choosing to counter the idea of "disadvantaged," and dismantle the deficit messaging created from misinformed perceptions and implicit biases. Building on the power levers of EP and RB, processes and practices are put in place that support the discovery of student value, strengths, and passions through which educators and students partner to develop skills and build agency guaranteeing a contribution and their pathway out of poverty. Respecting a student's culture and personal context, while helping them discover their strengths, empowers them to become agents of their own learning. Core to effectual instruction is an educator's understanding of their students' context as well as individual needs.

Working to dismantle generational cycles, cognitive impact, and deficit messaging as described helps provide access to a solid and equitable foundation for students and families to build on. The

22 Ponton, M. K., Schuette, C. T., & Confessore, G. J. (2009). An agentic perspective of self-directed learning as applied to children. *International Journal of Self-Directed Learning*, *6*(1), 46-58.

multiplied force and synergistic influence of these power levers work together to support the identified students and families countering the negative impacts. By embracing the paradigm shift and strength-based model from within the predecessor system of education we transform future systemic structures and help put an end to not only the school-to-prison pipeline and but other systemic inequities.

As leaders and practitioners, we understand that identifying and providing support is not enough to ensure sustainability, we must design and build for congruence.

**Design and Build for Coherence**

After assessing needs and taking action to execute and implement a strategy to disrupt the sources of fragmentation and misalignments, going forward we must design and build for congruency. First and foremost, the educational settings (school and classroom) require instructional delivery that is, as emphasized, considerate of the individual student. **Providing instruction and delivery of services that is out of sequence and developmentally inappropriate only serves to fragment learning and disrupt coherence.**

Although my assertion is that the solution to systemic inequities, like the issue of the school-to-prison pipeline, begins within the predecessor system of education, I am not saying that it is up to just those in education to get it done. It took stakeholders from many audiences to help run this in the ditch; it will take the same type of audience to contribute and commit to the reset.

Regardless of who you are, you can do something. The most powerful thing any of us can do – as we have repeated multiple times – is to pursue our own healing and then we will be in a position for greater impact. The last of the key drivers mentioned within UEP is multi-disciplinary. Multi-Disciplinary speaks to having all stakeholders at the table. We can't continue to put this on the shoulders of the educators and staff. They need to know they have support from the inside out, from state, district, and school leaders, as well as business and community partners.

**State, district and school leaders**. School leaders need the support of their district leaders and educators and staff need the support of their school leaders and on top of that district leaders need to know that the State Education Agency has their back. We all must commit to the authentic and integrous implementation of programming that supports an equitable reset. It is past time to step up to the plate and do the hard work of identifying areas within your comprehensive delivery of services that are fragmented and incongruent. In addition, making sure you are addressing internally and externally – among all stakeholders—mindsets that would perpetuate the fragmentation and incongruence. Staff members need to be equipped and supported, trained in critical areas that support successful implementation and sustainability of equitable, congruent delivery of educational services. It is long overdue to ensure a process is in place for Intentional and effectual engagement of parents and families. No more lip service and misappropriated funds. We need to consider broadening the role of teacher/educator, with the autonomy needed, to be more inclusive of a facilitator-coach that teaches. This shift speaks to the reciprocity and partnership between the student and teacher away from someone who has been conditioned to dispense "knowledge". This results in lifting a load and burden from the teacher they should have never been expected to carry. Imagine being judged for failing to squeeze a Size 12 into a Size 2. That's not accountability—that's distortion. We must provide the support for educators and staff, as they pursue coherence and meaning making in their own lives and in their practices.

**Business and community partners.** Failing schools are not good for community or business. Businesses and community members have an opportunity to partner with a school for the reset. If you can support a school in this way, some suggestions might be to engage a consultant to assess the systemic impact of trauma in their operations, funding training for educators and parents in the Neurosequential Modeling in Education (NME), Collaborative Problem Solving (CPS), or Compassionate Inquiry (CI), or better yet, all three. Perhaps you are a member of a larger association or network of like-hearted businesses or funders, you could bring awareness to that group and strengthen stakeholder support in the business community. Maybe you are a smaller business and can't fund a whole school effort and you decide to support a particular teacher, key position, or grade level. Finances are not the only assets; your time and expertise are invaluable and needed.

**Educators and school staff.** Educators need to make sure that they are exercising self-care. Self-care is a non-negotiable for educators. This is a prerequisite for your commitment to exercising empathy and building relationships inside the classroom. Based on the relationships and the understanding of your students, you can then provide context for their learning. This creates trust making students feel seen (*the same thing you want*) which leaves them with a sense of belonging (*the same thing you want).* All educators need to commit to understanding not only trauma symptoms and how they mimic other realities, but also trauma-resilient strategies. When you see children expressing maladaptive emotions and behaviors inconsistent with learning in the classroom, guard against responding negatively or in a punitive way and choose a restorative response instead. It is possible to be firm and loving at the same time.

Research tells that one of the ways to address emotional dysregulation is through the development of the frontal cortex. I call it "*The Educator's Bankshot*". "*The Educator's Bankshot*" is a cognitive positioning strategy for educators and practitioners that helps to facilitate the achievement of a desired goal; a strategy for recognizing and accessing the more. This strategy helps to navigate students past the place of pain to a place of purpose. It is predicated on healthy attachment and relationships in the classroom and learning environment. It uses techniques and strategies to maneuver past fears and anxiety (emotions and behaviors) to the front part of the brain (cognitive). Someone employing "*The Educator's Bankshot*" is committed to starting with the end in mind, finding a child's face in the future, and then partnering together to create the pathway to arrive there. When you anchor a student's learning to what is special about them it builds their confidence and self-efficacy and communicates that you care. To all the other stakeholders, **when educators know that**

**they are cared for, by those both inside and out, they are better able to express and reciprocate that care to their students.**

Moving forward, we not only identify and implement the strategies for dismantling the systems and processes that perpetuate this cycle but take on the personal responsibility of dismantling in our own lives, in our own hearts, and in our own minds. This requires hearts and minds willing to commit to the process of the reset, choosing daily connection instead of survival, choosing daily to push toward the greatest representation of self, and damning the voices that would tell you otherwise.

A commitment to reestablishing equitable foundations will bring an interrupt to the disproportionate misrepresentation in education for students. For this to happen, we need collaboration and capacity building with a network of partners, within and without, to create the model and ecosystem necessary to support the equitable reset. We can soothe our collective conscience with an ACE workshop, SEL training, or even restorative practices effort, but without courageous and reciprocal leadership committed to the reset, success will not be achieved. **Our practices, however, well-intended, are short-lived and potentially meaningless if the commitment to the integrity of the process is not there.**

Let's be honest. At the end of the day, we know exactly why things happen, why broken systems, and the systemic inequities they produce continue to exist. It is not that we do not know what to do. We know what to do. We just don't do what we know, and we don't do it in the right order.

What we get to do now is to identify the place of our dissatisfaction and then commit to the path of its correction. We can choose to reject justifying the means by the end. We can refuse to perpetuate the historical and generational trauma of the past and instead represent a collective committed to a reset in education that leads to healing and flourishing. I get it is BIG and feels overwhelming which sometimes makes it difficult to know where to begin but just begin.

# Chapter Four: The Plan

*Restoring Order through Identity and Integration*

## *Integrating the Reset*

1. What are the signs of a system—or a person—operating in "incongruence"?

2. What areas of your life are siloed or lacking integration?

3. How does a trauma-resilient organization treat integration differently than a compliance-driven one?

4. What specific structures in your school or workplace need to be reimagined to promote healing and order?

5. What does it look like to lead from a place of integrity and wholeness?

# CHAPTER FIVE
# THE PAYOFF

The last chapter describes the payoff of building trauma-resilient, equitable foundations in education. When we support regulated brains, elevate student agency, and build strong partnerships with families, schools begin to flourish. I highlight how this shift boosts educator capacity, strengthens programs, and improves outcomes across mental health, family life, and public systems. The ripple effects include economic growth, better health, and generational transformation. But it all starts with personal healing—coherence begins within. When students understand and own their stories, they don't just succeed—they contribute. In this vision, education becomes a tool for justice, wholeness, and societal flourishing.

# CHAPTER FIVE
# THE PAYOFF

Well, that was a lot. The last four chapters have been a summative share and view, you could say, of my lived experience and work to this point. In this last chapter, we will discuss the payoff of dare attempting the reestablishing of sound and equitable foundations in a system gone wrong. When we can be honest of where we are, while simultaneously seeing where we want to go, we can begin to map the steps forward.

To help us move forward collectively and personally, we will take time to engage in the practice of superimposing onto a future state. According to Walidah Imarisha, visionary fiction is "*fantastical literature that helps us to understand existing power dynamics and helps us imagine paths to creating more just futures.*" I would add, in the context of this conversation, it helps build paths toward coherence.

I will cast one and maybe you have another.

**Assets-based students using their story as their guide for learning, all from the place of secure environments and with regulated brains — finding, building, discovering, and contributing to their world ensuring equitable foundations and flourishing futures.**

When we learn to reverse engineer by remediating the system and countering the effects on the student, we will shift the foundation from inequitable to equitable.

**Equitable institutions are where leaders observe and recognize places of limitations and barriers, then stop to discern, and differentiate between suspected inabilities and their mimicking counterparts of developmental incapacities not yet matured or exercised.** As a result of this commitment to the shift needed, and learning on purpose, the future state begins to come into view.

A system reordered with equitable foundations cognizant of trauma-resilient practices, strategies, and processes to make it individually and collectively impactful is a system that creates outcomes that influence society and economies.

When this happens, school and learning environments go from fragmentation to integration. Imagine intentional and incentivized opportunities for integration. Trauma-resilient strategies and processes that help strengthen and regulate the emotions and the cognitive processing opening the space for healthier relationships with self and with others.

Through the intentional and incentivized efforts to close the gaps, we are building capacity and putting an end to mislabeling, replacing labels with compassion, recognizing trauma's systemic roots.

When we find ourselves in trauma-resilient environments, safety, growth mindset, positive expectations, and discovery are all a part of the daily landscape. An environment where equity in practice is exercised, curiosity is all the buzz and critical judgment on perceived deficits are questioned.

When we do the work of rebuilding capacity and agency, we go from surviving to thriving. **Oh, the joy, when the story is told.** When we can identify and address the interruption, we will then be able to uncover and discover the individualized intellect of the child that leads to their engagement and ownership of learning. A learning they can build on and develop into their signature contribution to the world. Fulfillment and wellbeing will be the order of the day. Putting children first, creating an environment and atmosphere that facilitates the telling of their story – now that's what I call education.

When you are operating from coherence and with the trauma-resilient strategies and processes in place to maintain it, the result is increased longevity and sustainability of programming and an increase in met goals.

Schools begin to recognize an increase in available monies and productivity through aligning deliverables across funding streams. As this occurs, wasted valuable time and redundant and fragmented work become a thing of the past.

When you feel and see that your efforts are making a visible difference, this has a direct impact on morale and job satisfaction. The health of teams goes up and buy-in increases with a welcome to accountability and expectation. All stakeholders pushing in the same direction provides synergy and momentum that can bring increase in every area.

The direct impact and benefit to the educator is big. With equitable load distribution and increased capacity, educators are better positioned to facilitate the success of students. They find the bandwidth to ensure activities and instruction that help regulate the brain are embedded into the programming of the day further reducing the weight dysregulated brains (cognitive, emotional, behavioral) in the classroom can create.

When you are working with regulated brains, your work becomes more consistent, solutions begin to show results, and you are not running from one initiative to the next, looking for what is going to stick. You are working from a solid foundation (*because you did the groundwork of creating paths of coherence*) from which to build long-standing success.

Schools and classrooms become welcoming places for parents. Being intentional about engaging parents and families in their child's education strengthens them to take ownership and equips them to be a more engaged school partner, sharing that weight, as they should, with the school. Students with regulated brains and parents who are engaged in their learning are children who are more cognitively positioned to learn. An increase in parent engagement, positively impacts the efficacy and effectiveness of student programming.

Parents and families partnering with their child's school as a result, in part, to the increased confidence in the child's success, but also the residual impact and increased confidence of the success of the family unit. They see themselves as interrupting generational cycles and that makes them feel good. Healthier and stronger families translate into healthier and stronger communities. A shift in perspective on learning and its impact on all of life can motivate parents to go back and address some of the areas where they may have had trouble in the past.

Fixed mindsets stuck in deficit messaging begin to shift to engage in growth mindset and the belief and expectation that ALL students can learn. The turnaround and upswing in student success resulting from a regulated brain will speak loudly to the school community dismantling belief systems that some kids just can't learn. Students begin to take ownership in their learning, understanding that the learning is for the facilitation of their contribution, not an academic exercise with no context. Providing students with an education that is respective of their person is an innovation that multiplies downstream impacting their individual economy as well as the larger one.

When the people inside the school shift perspective and that spills over into the community, this will begin to attract interest and investment. **Business and community partners recognizing that education is a social enterprise with social impact worthy of a social investment.** Being able to connect the beginning (regulated brains) to the end (successful learners reaching academic goals) has a direct impact on the wellbeing and the economy of society.

Not only is UEP a social pedagogy and what is needed to bring a reset in education, impacting everything downstream, it is a preventative measure to the mental and public health crisis. The cost avoided by addressing the issue of unresolved trauma early and with an integrative approach, as described herein, even with the mitigation of the cost added to resolve the trauma, will produce immeasurable results felt downstream — families, communities, workplace, mental and public health, economies — and on an exponential scale.

When we realize that economics is a function of education, and we engage in the application of a circular economy within this predecessor system to reduce and eliminate waste, investing it back into our most valuable asset — our students and their families — the outcome will be human flourishing that leads to positive social change and unbounded economic prosperity.

## Let's Start at the Very Beginning, it's a Very Good Place to Start

We end where we started and that is with you and me. Experiencing this shift in education and reestablishing equitable foundations begins with creating our own personal paths of coherence. What is the payoff to your own personal healing? Future casting from a personal perspective looks like getting back to essence or at least for starters making a commitment to its pursuit.

It looks like addressing the unresolved trauma hidden away and unpacking so you can begin to see ahead and clearly. **Unpacking**

**gives the gift to self that says you are worth my staying awhile.** The daily choices to endure momentary pain or discomfort because you know that better is on the other side. You know lasting fulfillment – being good with self - is better than fleeting "happiness".

It is about understanding that you will never be able to bring the wholeness or justice to the external until you begin to possess peace in the internal.

In your journey and pursuit of your best self, you realize that there is nothing wasted. One day you wake up and recognize that the trauma that you once allowed to victimize you is now serving you. It has become the path you are running on and is a problem you were born to solve. Retribution of an angry kind gets swallowed up in redemption of the best kind. This is the law of just return at work.

This release of pain and anger begins to shift the literal vibrational frequency in your body bringing your systems back into balance. Where there used to be fragmented and siloed processing coherence begins to come. The positive messaging and environments that are a result of this personal pursuit are taken in by the magnificent creative design called the brain. Your brain, in turn, sends the messages out to all other systems in the body. All the parts working together as they were designed to work.

Future casting on a personal level is the raised consciousness that there is more to know that you ever realized or imagined possible. You are amazed to find out that the truth you thought you knew was not all the truth there was to know. Suddenly, your capacity has expanded, along with your abilities. This is where generational cycles are interrupted, and deficit messaging ceases. The LOST child has been found and being in the NOW is a reality.

And just like you and I, every student carries a story. Education's call is not to erase it, but partner to reveal it.

When we use story as guide for learning, we find healing in the curriculum, flourishing becomes the measure, and the outcome is students and families bringing their best self to bear on the world around them. This is where we will find the key to education's reset and a society's healing.

# Chapter Five: The Payoff

## *Casting Vision and Reaping the Return of Restoration*

"One day you recognize the trauma that once victimized you is now serving you. It has become the path you are running on and is the problem you were born to solve."

— Dr. Ivy Bonk

### *Integrating the Reset*

1. How do regulated brains, engaged parents, and secure environments form the foundation of thriving students?

2. What does healing look like for you—not just emotionally, but economically, socially, relationally?

3. How does redefining education as a social enterprise shift how we design, fund, and assess it?

4. Why is it revolutionary to see Universal Equity Pedagogy as *preventative measure* for mental and public health?

5. How can you begin to cast a new vision—not just for schools, but for your family, your city, your legacy?

# APPENDIX

## Integrating the Reset

At the end of each chapter, you will find a section called ***Integrating the Reset***. These reflective questions are for deeper processing and application. Think of them as doorways—ways of moving from passive reading into active integration, where ideas shift from words on a page into practices shaping your own story, community, and work. Ways to use:

**Personal Reflection:** Journal your responses. Allow yourself the freedom to write honestly and without judgment. You may discover insights that surface only when you give yourself space to linger on the question.

**Dialogue**: Use the questions in conversation with a trusted friend, colleague, or small group. Sharing your perspectives and hearing others' creates new connections and helps uncover blind spots.

**Organizational Practice**: For leaders or teams, the questions can serve as prompts for staff meetings, retreats, or strategy sessions. They can spark dialogue that surfaces hidden assumptions and invites new ways of structuring work.

**Ongoing Revisit**: The same question may invite different responses at different times. Return to them later—after a decision, transition, or season of growth—and notice what has shifted in you.

The purpose is not simply to answer, but to allow the questions to do their work in you: stretching, unsettling, inspiring, and grounding. In this way, ***Integrating the Reset*** becomes less about completing an exercise and more about cultivating a practice of transformation.

## Look for Reset on Deck

***Reset on Deck*** is a professional learning card game designed to help schools and educators explore and apply the principles of Universal Equity Pedagogy (UEP). Using a set of 22 custom icons, the game challenges participants to recognize patterns of fragmentation, problem blindness, and misaligned practices while practicing shifts toward coherence, equity, and trauma-resilient strategies.

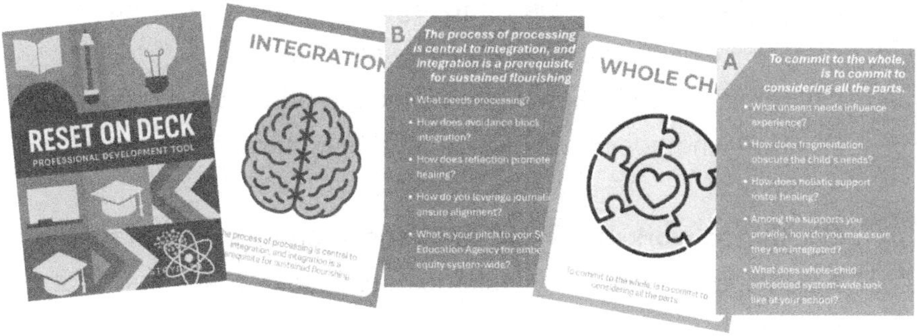

# Let Us Help

*Education's Reset and a Society's Healing* is a blueprint for transformation; a vision for what's possible when equity, coherence, and healing are woven into the fabric of our systems. But every school, district, or community carries its own story—and we must honor that uniqueness. That's where Rethink Learning, Inc. (www.rethinklearning.org) comes in. Dr. Ivy Bonk and the collective of social impact strategists at RTL would love to partner with you whether you are in education, nonprofits, community organizations, or government agencies to create tailored integration and implementation strategies that bring the "new" to life in practical, sustainable ways.

Whether you are looking for:

- **Support in drafting policy and legislation** to embed equity, coherence, and sustainability at systemic levels
- **Customized roadmaps** that adapt these principles to your setting—whether classrooms, entire districts, or cross-sector coalitions
- **Facilitated workshops and trainings** to engage educators, staff, parents, and community stakeholders in shared ownership of change
- **Implementation coaching and capacity-building** to ensure efforts take root and endure over time
- **Bridge-building strategies** that connect schools, families, and community partners for collective impact

The new is not a one-size-fits-all solution. It's a framework that comes alive through your people, your culture, and your story. We would love to hear how you are creating paths of coherence in your work and how we might help.

**imreadyforthereset@rethinkinglearning.org**

Made in the USA
Monee, IL
04 November 2026

67383310R00085